THE SIMPLE MAGICK OF WILD THINGS
THE JOURNEY OF A SOUTHERN MALE WYTCH

THE SIMPLE MAGICK OF WILD THINGS

THE JOURNEY OF A SOUTHERN MALE WYTCH

DAVE GADDY

FOREWORD BY
JAKE RICHARDS

ARABI MANOR
A REBEL SATORI IMPRINT
New Orleans & New York

Published in the United States of America by
Rebel Satori Press
www.rebelsatoripress.com

Book design: Sven Davisson

Paperback ISBN: 978-1-60864-288-5

This book is dedicated to the legacy of Cindy Maluna, a true wytch of wisdom.
It is dedicated to her magickal spirit, which continues to inspire and guide us
on our journeys. May her light forever dance
in the realms of the ancients.

ACKNOWLEDGEMENTS

I would like to express my heartfelt gratitude to all who made this book possible. To Jay, you have been a guiding light through this process. To my family for their unwavering support and encouragement through this journey. In this book, I honor the memories of each of those who have passed from this realm, and I am thankful to Ma and Pop and each niece and nephew. Brittanie, Stephanie, Dakotah, Bentley, Dominic, Walker, Devin, Haven, and Damien…you add your own special magick to every day of my life. To my friends, who provided valuable insights and inspiration. Donna Elizabeth, Jackie Knapp, Cheryl Hill, Ethan Black, Justin Hughes, Madolyn Locke, Jerry Pound, Jason Williams, Rev. Laura Gonzalez, Frater Aaron, Christopher Aaron Todd, and Curt Tice…you have helped me to see the laughter, love, and magick in each moment and each footprint of my journey. To my dedicated editor and the publishing team, Sven and the team at Rebel Satori Press and Arabi Manor, for their expertise and guidance. You have believed in me and supported me from the beginning. To the countless individuals whose stories and experiences have enriched the pages of this book. And finally, to you, the readers, for your time and curiosity. I hope this book offers you knowledge, inspiration, and, more than anything, magick.

CONTENTS

FOREWORD

Jake Richards

When I first met Dave, I knew it was evident that he was a storyteller, telling stories of those who no longer can. Stories of people he loved and cherished, and who helped build him as a man. He is such a delight to speak to, and such a sweet person. He is also a person who speaks their truth, both for others and for himself, regardless. Dave invited me on a podcast to talk about ancestral stories and to share my own, and during the process we just talked and talked about our upbringings and our elders, finding similarities in our southern boy childhoods. I think we clicked because like Dave, I was very close to my elders, especially my grandmother. She was my best friend, and reading the following book and seeing how fondly he spoke of his time with his Mamaw touched my heart so much. I think the only love second to that of a mother and child is that of a grandmother and her grandchildren.

Before I touch on the work to follow, I figured I would introduce myself for those unaware. I was born and raised in the mountainous corner of upper East Tennessee, spending many childhood adventures in the mountains and forests of Southwestern Virginia, East Tennessee, and Western North Carolina. My family has been here for generations, either tilling the soil for crops, hauling lumber, or working in the mills. I was raised by my mama and her mother for the majority of my life. They caredd for me and my sister, and then when the time came, we cared for my grandmother, and we all danced through the dementia with her. She was my best friend and the hardest sting death has had on my heart. So thank you, Dave, for walking me down those memories.

I am an Appalachian conjure man and folk healer, titles no one wishes to really bare, but one which arises out of necessity of the community and the horned gifts given you by God and the spirits. See, back in the day it was believed that certain children are born with gifts of the Sight and the power to do things. The circumstances of such births usually occurred as either mother or child, or both, passed through the grips of death, whether this was a breeched birth, c-section, born with a caul over the face, or born after the mother had already passed. Other times it had to do with the day and time one was born, whether during a thunderstorm, at the strike of midnight, on Christmas Day, and so on.

With me, I was born blue. I inhaled the fluids before I was born, and that was my "first breath" as I was told. Growing up, my childhood was much like any other boy who grew up in the country: trying each year to fill your daddy's water wading boots while fishing, playing in the creek on the mountain in North Carolina, or running through my grandfather's corn and sunflowers at the base of the Unicoi Mountains; catching lightning bugs on warm July nights while hearing stories about how they can be souls of returning loved ones or heading to play in the woods along with Nana's warning to head on home if you hear a woman screaming cause it could be a painter (a panther or mountain lion).

I grew up in a spiritual home, one that spoke of angels walking through rooms that suddenly become quiet or of the haints that will leave greasy handprints on the walls bigger than anyone's in the house, along with the possibility of an extra finger of the print as well. Our lives were tied to the seasons, and we lived by them. When Dogwood winter began, and the dogwoods began to bloom after a small cold spell, it was time to clean house. I'd wake up on weekend mornings to mama scrubbing the walls and doors and other general cleaning while the open front door and windows brought in a circulation of fresh spring air, getting rid of the dense cave-like air that it had become from us being huddled up.

And then summer would come, and it was time to start helping the elders break beans and start canning for the next seasons to come. And then fall would announce her arrival, and we'd head out to collect walnuts in big apple baskets to sell at the flea market for some extra money, along with the copper wire daddy had spent days stripping and burning. These events and ventures were of course not assigned any particular date, but by the season and the feel of the mountain air itself, as if the need and want to begin rose up in their spirits like sap rising up in the trees.

That's how we lived by and *with* the land and it's other inhabitants. We've always known that the flora and fauna of the land can teach us about life, whether it be the resourcefulness of the chickadee nest to teach us about our home life or observing a fox move her kits to higher ground away from the river, a sign that a big rain was coming. Even with all this "connectedness," rural America still has its issues, especially in the South throughout history. Today, these ancestral sins and struggles still linger in families, communities, and southern society, whether it be mental health issues, alcoholism, drug use, racism, fatalism, food insecurity, poverty, chronic illness, and abuse of natural resources either to get by until the next month or under a corporate hand. These things affect us knowingly or unknowingly through generations on a community scale and an individual scale.

And in the modern day, it's our job to address, rectify, and break those generational sins and cycles. And the following book is just for that, the first of its kind that I'm aware of. If you're looking for a recipe book or an easy how-to guide on southern magic to get what you want, then this ain't it. Instead, Dave leads you down his own story of finding the magic of the South in his blood and bones, in the moss and creeks. And then he invites you to do the same in exercises at the end of each chapter, and who better to help guide us down these paths than those who first paved them under the need for survival and making the world manageable than your own ancestors? While we seek the guidance of our ancestors, though, Dave subtly reminds us that the most important guide and opinion for our path is ourselves. We are the ones living in this world today and walking these roads, and it is on our shoulders that the generational baggage is laid. And it is our decision what to do with it, to either leave it behind or work through the baggage and continue to carry it with us as a part of our story. Because our story begins at the end of theirs, and theirs began with the end of those before even them, and on and on it goes.

Reading this book of stories and adventures, traumas and joys, reminded me of my own story. Of my elders before me, of their laughs and queer ways of doing things, and ways that I see them within myself, physically and characteristically. It made me long for home-places now long gone, now sheltering some other family or now joined to the earth it once stood on, with the only witnesses to the magic of life and love there now being the mountains and rolling waters.

But Dave also reminds us that we need to claim and embrace their strengths as well, learning to face the world head-on as they did while giving pity and comfort to those who weren't able to do so. So, in this way, we do it for all of them: facing the world and its issues and the issues within ourselves, hand in hand with those who did the same, and in honor of those who couldn't find the strength to. It's become a sort of cliché phrase, "We are our ancestors", but I think people miss the major meaning of it. We're not exactly them, but we are made up of them. We share laugh lines with some, and with others, we share talents, likes and dislikes, and maybe even trauma. In working on ourselves, we become the best of them and more so, healing divides created so many lives ago, and fixing things we didn't break so no one gets cut anymore. We elevate them in spirit through this, and by doing this, we certify and more clear and healed path for those to come.

Dave also introduces us to our neighbors on the land, the *Wildlings*, as he calls them. Through this, Dave reminds us how the natural world can teach us acceptance of ourselves and circumstances we find ourselves in, as well as acceptance of ourselves. To learn silence and peace, to accept allowance for the ways we sometimes get in our own ways. But most importantly to not only find the magic in ourselves, but also in all those faces we meet everyday. And through this we begin to see ourselves as our ancestors lived and toiled, passing from one season to the next, being as prepared as can be, but if not, facing it all head on with the sounds of hundreds of footsteps behind us. And when you take that step, that next step in a long line of steps on a journey full of love and crying, praying and mourning, big family gatherings and solitude in a barn with a rope… then you continue a path you didn't start, a path that needs clearing of briars and sharp stones and deep holes. You continue the journey of magic through the years and home places, through the forests and fields alight with fireflies. You begin the journey of a *Southern Wytch*.

INTRODUCTION

"Hello there, fellow traveler. I guess this is where I introduce myself properly – I go by the name of Dave Gaddy, The Weathered Wiseman. This book I've put together is called *The Simple Magick of Wild Things*, and it's a humble offering to those who seek to explore the magick that you can find in the everyday.

I know that right off there are going to be those who want to know why I use the spelling 'Wytch' and 'Magick.' The short answer is because I like them. The word 'Wytch,' according to the English Dictionary is an obsolete form of the word 'witch.' It was used by some folks as the title for a male witch. The reason I like the spelling of the word 'Magick' is because, for me, the spelling 'Magic' always represented slight of hand or stage magic and I love that 'Magick' can be used to describe my own personal practices. So there really is no rocket science or religious debate. I just like those spellings.

I was born and raised in North Carolina, but I currently call Atlanta, Georgia home. I spend a big part of my time wandering the woods just beyond the edge of the house, where the song of the wind and the rustle of leaves are some of my dearest friends. You see, I've always believed that magick isn't so much about fireworks and fanciful displays. It's about the quiet moments, the natural world, and the wisdom that's woven into that existence.

I grew up on dirt roads, the kind that snaked their way through the countryside, connecting one pasture to another. It was a humble life, one where the rhythms of the seasons dictated our days.

The roads were often muddy in the spring, making it a game to navigate them without getting stuck. But those same roads were also lined with wildflowers, their colors stretching as far as the eye could see, painting the landscape with the promise of new beginnings.

Summer brought sweltering heat, and the roads were dusty under the relentless sun. We'd kick up clouds of dirt as we played, chasing lightning bugs and enjoying the freedom of long, lazy days.

Fall was a symphony of colors as the leaves turned brilliant shades of red and gold. The dirt roads became a tunnel of foliage, a passage into a world of magick and wonder. We'd walk those roads, crunching leaves underfoot, feeling the earth's heartbeat beneath us.

And then there was winter when the dirt roads turned into a mix of frost, mud, and ice. The world turned quiet, and we'd bundle up in layers of clothing, our boots crunching on the frozen ground as we explored the icy wonderland.

Life on those dirt roads was a simple one. We learned the value of hard work and the importance of community. Neighbors helped neighbors, and the bond between us was as strong as the earth itself.

As I look back on those days, I realize that the dirt roads of my childhood were more than just a means of getting from place to place. They were a symbol of a way of life, one that was rooted in the land and in the connections we forged with each other. Those dirt roads, with their mud, dust, and potholes, taught me the beauty of simplicity and the power of the land to shape our lives and our hearts.

Now, you might wonder, 'What's this book all about?' Well, it's a bit like a fireside chat with an old friend. It's about reconnecting with the Earth, telling stories, and making friends with the wild creatures that share this land. It's about discovering the magick hidden in plain sight, right under our noses.

In this book, we'll be taking a leisurely stroll through the woods, reminiscing about kinfolk long-gone, sharing stories, and learning the language of the land. It's an invitation to slow down, to find beauty in simplicity, and to remember that we, too, are part of the natural world's makeup.

So, go ahead and find yourself a cozy corner, brew a cup of tea or coffee, and let's embark on this journey together. *The Simple Magick of Wild Things* is a testament to the magick that's within reach, if only we have the eyes to see and the heart to believe. Welcome, my dear friend, to a world where the whispers of nature hold the keys to our own magick.

CHAPTER ONE
DEEP FRIED AND DIRT
GROWN

"I am a southern male wytch, deep fried and dirt grown. Growing
up in this unique blend of culture and magick has made me who
I am today. Just as the south is known for its rich flavors and
hospitality, I've found a deep richness in the world of wytchcraft,
where intuition, nature, and spirituality intertwine. Like the secret
recipe for a beloved dish, my path as a wytch is my own personal
journey, filled with family traditions and the magick of the land. So,
I embrace who I am, rooted in my heritage and the legacy of those
before me."

For as long as I can remember, I have always traveled dirt roads and wandered into areas that others may or may not go. I was born and raised in
rural North Carolina. Most of my kin were farm folks or country folks
with little to no education and lives steeped in superstition and folklore. I
wasn't a bad child....just mischievous. I was the one who, if dared, would
try anything once (I am still very much like this, just for clarification).

I remember when I was 8 or so, we were visiting my Grandma's farmhouse in Fairfield, NC. There was no indoor plumbing and no running
water. If you needed to use the bathroom, you used the outhouse located
close to the pasture. My aunt, who, incidentally, was not a small woman,
had to use the facilities. She went outside, closed the door, and got settled

in. I had happened to find a small green snake while I was outside playing and thought it could be fun to feed it through a hole in the outhouse wall so that my aunt could see him. I remember vividly the screams that emanated from that outhouse as that little green snake flicked its tongue over my aunt's left buttcheek. That door burst open, and my aunt is standing there with her pants around her ankles and her face red with fury. I knew that I needed to run as hard and as fast as I could to avoid any repercussions. I took off across the pasture with my aunt flying as hard as her legs would go, with her underwear and pants twisting around her ankles as she ran. I remember seeing her trip and roll on the ground a few times with her backside showing for all the rest of the kin and cousins to see in all its glory. She chased me for what seemed like days, but when I finally got tired enough to get caught, I got the beating of my life….but….it was completely worth it. Entertainment wasn't easily accessible for country folk.

I was also a very curious child. If you asked my Ma, she would say it was more nosiness than curiosity. There was an old abandoned house just across the railroad tracks from where we lived. I was obsessed with this house. It had an amazing and eerie energy about it. Even at the age of 8 or 10, I could already sense and discern energies. My dad tended to encourage the natural curiosities with the unusual that I possessed. He would often go with me to explore that house. It seems like only yesterday that I was standing in that old dilapidated living room with the worn-out furniture that squirrels and other varmints had made homes and nests in. As I stood there looking at all the years of neglect and abandonment, I heard someone call my name. I didn't think much of it…it was probably my dad. I went looking for him to see what he wanted. I found him outside and asked why he called me. Of course, he said that he had been outside the whole time and hadn't called my name at all. Most kids would be freaked out by this. Not me. What did I do? I went back into the living room and tried to talk to whoever called me. Of course, that was when Pop decided it was time to head back home.

I was always that kid who explored the woods or tried to talk to a wild animal. I spent many a weekend in the woods behind our house on Walkup Avenue talking to squirrels and birds and even the occasional skunk. Thankfully, they never felt threatened enough with me to spray. I think of how close I probably was, too many times, to getting skunked.

Growing up in NC, we always lived close to family and I only lived in three different houses throughout my childhood. The first was the house that my great-grandpa and great-grandma lived in on Walkup Avenue. The second was a small house on Colony Road with a big backyard; the last was in the country close to Waxhaw. In those three places, I found respite from the pressures of trying to play it straight when I truly wasn't. I knew that I was different in so many ways even before I knew what gay and wytchy was.

My friends were always the local wildlife or the farm animals (either the ones we had or my grandma's). My dad's mom was one of my biggest cheerleaders and also a bit of an instigator. Both of my grandmas play a big part in who I have grown into. My dad's mom (we called her MawMaw), was always bigger than life. She was full of energy, feisty, and loved to laugh and have fun. I always said that she should have been an entertainer and one of her joys was living life through me. She taught me to sing and play guitar as soon as I could make a noise or hold the guitar. As she would cook, she played the radio and when a song that she liked came on, she would start prancing toward me, rocking her hips and moving her feet. She loved to dance and would do so at the drop of a hat. There were many Saturday nights in my teen years that she would call me and have me come get her and we would both head to the square dance in Waxhaw. Even in her 80's the woman could outdance me and did so with so much gusto.

MawMaw lived down the hill from an old cemetery. I still remember thinking that with her having well water, I wonder who all ended up in the drinking water. I still remember the day my mama asked me why I only drank store-bought drinks with no ice at my granny's house. When I told her that I really wasn't too fond of the idea of drinking down old cousin Bessie, I thought she was going to spit her tea right then. It was after that day that my mother stopped drinking my granny's water and wouldn't use ice in any of her store-bought drinks there.

I would spend many a summer wandering that old dirt road up to that cemetery and staring at the tombstones wondering who these people were and what kinds of lives they led. Those summers would be spent with something in my hand straight from the garden....typically a nice vine ripe tomato or even a turnip. I would rinse it off in the creek and gnaw on it as I explored and I was typically in overalls and no shirt and barefoot. Yeah... I'm not a hick at all.

My MawMaw loved to laugh. She was one that threw laughter around easily and willingly. I will always remember the one phrase that she kept on the tip of her tongue when people wanted to live in the pain and misery of daily life, "Hon, I reckon the Good Lord up there ain't just up for serious business all the time. Not at all...He sprinkled a whole lot of laughing dust around these parts, because He knew that life was way too short to keep that grin hidden. So, go on now shug, let that nose wrinkle up, let your belly laughs roll....because up in them heavenly hills and highways, the Good Lord and them angels love hearing that type of earthly music."

Now believe me, MawMaw had her tribulations (as the old folk called them). MawMaw was 8 years old when her own mama died. Her dad, Marshall, remarried two or three years later, and there were 9 more kids born from that marriage. MawMaw wasn't one to dwell on the hard times, and there were many. She believed that you had to have fight in you and that if you cried too much, it was a waste of energy. I think that is why she sang and danced and played instruments.   She always believed that if you kept the mind and the body busy, that trouble wouldn't stay too long.

I don't know that the way MawMaw lived her life would be considered 'wytchcraft,' so to speak. With her, everything was done on an 'as needed' basis. That need may have been met with a poultice or a tonic or whistle to the wind. Most often, one of the Psalms would accompany anything she did. I will always remember growing up, no matter whose house you visited; there was always that huge brick of a family bible sitting out in the middle of the living room. It was full of family pictures and trees and pressed plants and flowers. MawMaw's old bible wasn't the exception. I remember one of the first times I went to pick it up…she came running over to make sure none of the 'blessings' would fall out. I think that is one of the teachings I hold onto to this day. "Be careful how you hold onto things; the blessings might fall out."

That lesson alone has guided me in how I try to live my life around other people. I look at all the hurt and pain in the world today, and I think that some folk need to be handled a little tenderly…they are trying to keep what blessings they have and keep them from spilling out. They need that extra bit of love….they need a smile and a reason to laugh.

Because of MawMaw, I have always taken on the role of clown and caretaker all at the same time. I learned at an early age that if you laugh at yourself first, it takes all the ammo out of someone else's hands. Let me tell you, being a fat, gay, wytchy child presented lots of opportunity for bullying…especially living in the country, but through the lessons MawMaw taught me, I was able to look those bullies in the eyes and show them that there was more to me than met the eye.

Another thing MawMaw taught me was how to 'scrap', as she called it. MawMaw would never think of backing down from a fight. I watched her as her last husband (who was an alcoholic with a violent nature) threatened her one night. He starts toward her and me with fists balled up. MawMaw didn't miss a beat. She reached over to the closest end table and picked up one of her lead crystal ashtrays, looked him dead in the eyes and told him, "Try to lay a finger on either one of us and the ambulance will be hauling your cold, dead body out of this house with my good ashtray stuck in your skull."

I also watched this strong, southern woman in her eighties beat the living tar out of my aunt Genelle at the senior citizen center back home. Every Thursday night, they hosted a type of tea dance for the seniors in the area and both MawMaw and my aunt Genelle (actually my aunt on my mom's side) were part of their frequent flyers group. Of course, both of these women liked their men, and they both had their sights set on one old fellow in particular. Turns out that MawMaw had been 'seeing' him for a few weeks already, but aunt Genelle had designs on making him hers. I watched as these two put together women smacked and yelled and pulled hair and even threw punches. By the end of it, MawMaw didn't have a scratch on her but aunt Genelle looked like she had been beaten with a briar bush and hobbled out of the senior center defeated and bruised. You don't mess with a Southern woman and her male friends.

Of course, I got every bit of MawMaw's piss and vinegar. When I started my freshman year of high school, I was jumped in the hall one morning by a senior. He picked me up by my throat and pushed me up against the wall with both feet dangling at least a foot off the floor. I can still see the anger in his eyes as he yelled out, 'Who do you think you are, you faggot. I saw you staring at me." In that moment, the only thing I could think of was survival. I knew that if I let him keep the upper hand, that I was done for. I looked him in the eyes and told him that I wasn't the least bit scared of him (I learned from the animals I grew up with that if you showed fear or pain when you were threatened, you might as well give up). I pulled my foot up and, with every ounce of strength I had, laid the hardest kick I could to his crotch. I dropped from the wall but was able to gain my balance. I looked at him crumpled on the floor and told him that if he ever did it again, I would make sure he couldn't use those parts ever again.

I don't condone violence by any means. Still, I also learned a long time ago from a wise and strong-willed woman that you don't just take everything that is handed to you; sometimes you have to fight, and you have to show the world that you've got gumption and the determination to see your way through those tribulations.

My teenage years were surrounded by farmers, rednecks, and lots of country folks. My best friend used to tell me that I was the toughest, funniest gay hick he had ever met. I take that as a full-on compliment. I try to live up to that reputation every day of my life. When I look at my family tree, I see centuries of strong country folk who had to fight to survive. When my ancestors came over from Scotland, they were sharecroppers and preachers with a strong sense of family…and that family dynamic came in all forms. You watch out for each other, make each other laugh, sing together, and dance through the difficult times.

In these days, it may be harder to find that song and dance, but it is there. You may need to dig a bit to find them, but there is magick in the trials. MawMaw was a living example of her favorite bible verses, 2 Corinthians 4:8,9, 16;18….she recited it often when trouble reared its head, "We are hard pressed on every side, but not crushed; perplexed, but not in despair; persecuted, but not abandoned; struck down, but not destroyed. Therefore, we do not lose heart. Though outwardly we are wasting away, yet inwardly, we are being renewed day by day. For our light and momentary troubles are achieving for us an eternal glory that far outweighs them all. So we fix our eyes not on what is seen but on what is unseen. For what is seen is temporary, but what is unseen is eternal."

My life has been touched by magick in so many ways. I have been fortunate enough to always have the love and support of my family, no matter what the circumstances might be. MawMaw never said she was a wytch… never felt the need to put a title to it. She just did things and knew things. She always had a sparkle in her eyes, and you never really knew if she was up to something or if she was just feeling feisty. Most of the time it was a mix of the two. There was always food on the table and good conversation. MawMaw never met a stranger (Ma says that my Pop and I both got that gene), and she tried her best not to make judgment on anyone. "Everybody has their own story, and it is up to us to help them write it with the happiest ending they can make."

MawMaw had a way of making you feel at home no matter what you were going through or what stress you were feeling. Everything could be made better with a cup of coffee and a slice of whatever pie or cake she had made that morning. She would look at you with that sly little smile of hers and you knew that she was either going to make you sing with her, spontaneously break into a dance, or laugh with every ounce of elation you thought had disappeared.

MawMaw and I solved many a problem over a bucket of beans that needed to be strung and broken or peas that needed to be shelled. She would tell the stories of our kin and tell me how strength, laughter, and song were a natural part of who I was. She taught me that life holds many areas that will require compromise, but in the midst of that, to never compromise who I am. Deep Fried and Dirt Grown...those roots run deep, and I am fortunate that I am who I am because of the way I was raised. Deep Fried, I can withstand anything. When the heat of life presses down, I come out on the other side with a tough exterior but with a tenderness and adaptability that got my ancestors through the worst of times. Dirt Grown, I keep my feet planted in nature and hold to the roots of my ancestors. It is with determination, a strong heart, and yes, magick that we can be the writers of our own stories...never subjected to what others want to make us, but always the hero of our journey.

As a young man, the one thing that I tried to do was to leave my culture and who I was raised to be behind. My dreams were to leave my small town and to make something of myself. I did everything I could think of to abandon those hickish, old country pieces of myself and to become someone who was well-educated and would not be singled out because of my accent. My first year out of high school, I made the trek to New York City in pursuit of a career on Broadway. In the midst of this adventure, I managed to neutralize my southern drawl and carry myself as a 'worldly' soul.

I managed to be a working actor for a year, but it was exhausting. I felt that I was losing myself along the way. I longed to be back in the country and to see and feel trees and open fields. As I walked the streets of the city, I found myself heavy with melancholy, and I felt completely alone for the first time in my life. I didn't see leaving New York City as a failure. I went, and I did what I had set out to do. I had been a working actor for a season of my life. It was time to go back home.

Once I got home, I was amazed at how fast all of my work to lose my accent flew out the window. It came rushing back to me like an old friend. I have heard it said that you can't go home again. I didn't find that to be the case. I easily fell back into country life. I never regretted my time in the city, but I kept it tucked inside like a wonderful secret that only I knew.

Once I was back home, I fell back into everyday life with the chickens and the goats and, of course, Ma and Pop. At the time, I was also thrust into a parental role with my twin nieces. As I moved through day to day life, I was learning more about who I was and the direction my life would take. I don't think anything happens by accident, and I was willing to walk out each piece of the odyssey before me.

I learned more about who I am and what inspired passion in my spirit. It took quite a bit of soul searching and introspection to realize that who I am is the perfect balance of my past, present, and future and that I am the result of experience and circumstance and the strength and passions of my own kin. I have come to love my own southernness and the humor and the wild idiosyncrasies of my family and ancestors. We are a colorful crowd, and I am good with that. MawMaw always did say that being normal was overrated. As I get older, I realize that this is very true and that normal tends to be boring and very much non-magickal.

I am very much an old southern wytch now. I crave the mossy, dirty crevices of the woods. I long to be where the magick happens. I find my home in nature and among the spirits of those wonderful wild kin that came before. I have taken it on myself to rewrite my story and in that story there are many heroes…many magickal folk…and more magick than any book can hold.

Exercise: "Rewrite Your Story"

Objective: This exercise is designed to help you reflect on your life story, identify areas where you may want to make changes, and begin the process of rewriting your narrative to align with your goals and aspirations.

Materials Needed:
– Journal or notebook
– Pen or pencil
– Quiet, reflective space

Instructions:
1. Set the Scene:

   Find a quiet and comfortable space where you won't be disturbed. Take a few deep breaths to relax and clear your mind.

2. Reflect on Your Current Story:

   Write down the key elements of your life story as it stands today. This can include your background, upbringing, significant life events, and your self-perception. Be honest and open in your reflection.

3. Identify Areas for Change:

   Review what you've written and highlight or underline aspects of your story that you'd like to change or improve. These could be related to your personal life, career, relationships, or any other area.

4. Define Your Desired Story:

   Imagine the life story you want to create for yourself. What are your goals, dreams, and aspirations? How do you want to see yourself in the future? Write a clear and detailed description of your desired story.
5. Identify Steps Towards Change:

Break down the changes you want to make into smaller, actionable steps. What can you start doing today to move closer to your desired story? List these steps in your journal.

6. Create a New Narrative:

Rewrite your life story based on your desired outcomes and the steps you've identified. Craft a narrative that embodies the person you want to become.

7. Visualize the New Story:

Close your eyes and vividly visualize yourself living your new story. Imagine the feelings, experiences, and successes associated with this narrative. Let this visualization inspire and motivate you.

8. Commitment and Accountability:

Write a commitment statement in your journal, pledging to take the necessary actions to rewrite your story. Share this commitment with a trusted friend or mentor who can hold you accountable.

9. Regularly Review and Adjust:

Periodically revisit your journal, reviewing your progress and making adjustments to your narrative and action steps as needed. Celebrate your achievements along the way.

10. Practice Self-Compassion:

Remember that rewriting your story is a journey, and it's okay to encounter setbacks or challenges. Practice self-compassion and resilience as you work toward your desired narrative.

Let's Do the Working:

Ritual for Writing Your Own Story

Materials Needed:
- – Journal or paper
- – Pen or pencil
- – Candle (any color that resonates with you)
- – Comfortable and quiet space

Steps:

1. Setting the Space: Find a quiet and comfortable space where you won't be interrupted. Light the candle and place it in front of you. This symbolizes the illumination of your path as you write your own story.

2. Centering Yourself: Close your eyes, take a few deep breaths, and allow yourself to relax. Imagine yourself surrounded by a warm, protective light. Feel yourself grounded and ready to embark on this creative journey.

3. Defining Your Intention: Hold the pen or pencil in your hand and say aloud or in your mind, "I am ready to write my own story, to express my unique experiences, dreams, and desires."

4. Igniting the Imagination: Open your journal or take a piece of paper. Imagine the blank pages as a canvas where your story will unfold. Visualize the words flowing effortlessly from your heart to your hand.

5. Reflecting on Your Past: Take a few moments to reflect on your journey so far. What pivotal moments, challenges, and triumphs have shaped you? Write down the key events that have brought you to this point.

6. Embracing Your Present: Shift your focus to your current situation. What are your passions, aspirations, and values? What brings you joy and fulfillment? Write down your thoughts and feelings about where you are right now.

7. Dreaming Your Future: Envision the future you desire for yourself.

What goals do you want to achieve? What experiences do you wish to have? Write down your dreams, no matter how big or small.

8. Crafting Your Narrative: Begin writing your story. Let your words flow freely and authentically. Describe the challenges you've overcome, the lessons you've learned, and the growth you've experienced. Include your present circumstances and the exciting possibilities that lie ahead.

9. Affirming Your Journey: As you write, repeat affirmations such as "I am the author of my own story" or "I embrace the power to shape my life." Let these affirmations infuse your writing with positive energy.

This is a sample of what I have used in my own rituals:

"From the past's pages, I release the chains of old beliefs and limitations. Let them dissolve like ink in water, making way for new possibilities. Like a phoenix rising from the ashes, I embrace transformation and growth.

With each word I choose, I shape my destiny. I cast away doubt and fear, replacing them with courage and confidence. As the pen glides across the paper, I am the author of my own tale, painting my journey with colors of authenticity and purpose.

I reclaim my power to direct my life's course. Like a sculptor shaping clay, I mold my experiences with intention and mindfulness. Every thought and action becomes a brushstroke on the canvas of my existence.

By the flickering candle's light, I declare this spell to rewrite my story cast. As I put pen to paper, I embrace the authority to create the narrative that aligns with my heart's desires. So mote it be."

10. Expressing Gratitude: Close your eyes and take a moment to express gratitude for the experiences that have shaped you, the opportunities that lie before you, and the ability to write your own narrative.

11. Closing: Blow out the candle, knowing that you've ignited the spark of creativity within you. Thank the universe, your inner self, or any higher power you believe in for guiding you through this ritual.

12. Continuing the Journey: This ritual can be revisited whenever you

feel the need to connect with your own narrative. Your journal can become a sacred space to document your ongoing story, dreams, and growth.

Remember, you have the power to write your own story. Each word you put on paper is a step towards creating the life you envision.

CHAPTER TWO
DON'T LOOK IN THE POT

"Amid life's twists and turns, laugh out loud with all your strength.
Tell the stories that helped shape your soul. And when your heart
seeks warmth and comfort, cook those favorite dishes. For in these
simple moments, life's sweetest memories and some of the most
powerful magick is born."

Most visits with my grandma were adventures within themselves. I remember that Ma would tell me every time we went to her house for supper... "Don't look in the pot." As a little squirt, I took Ma at her word for years....scared that there might be some wild and wooly beast in that pot ready to jump out and rip me to shreds (the imagination of a 5 or 6-year-old was strong with this one). It actually turns out that my imagination wasn't all that far from the truth. One lazy Sunday, all of the kinfolk had come to my grandma's for a fish fry. My step-grandpa had drained the pond and was going to restock the fish.

It seems that whenever we had those fish fries, that the only fish that they could get was catfish. There never seemed to be enough trout or perch...only catfish. Out of all the fish I have eaten in my life, catfish is my least favorite. To this day, I haven't found anyone or anywhere that can soak the mud out of that fish. Anytime I have put a bite of it in my mouth, I taste dirt, mud, and anything else that fish has consumed in its lifetime.

Anyway, on that Sunday afternoon, curiosity got the best of me and I wanted to make sure that catfish wasn't the only option on the menu for that day. I waited until all the grownups had gone outside to gossip, horse laugh, and quench their thirst on strong, syrupy glasses of sweet tea. I moved up next to that old stove and the first pot I opened....safe. It was catfish stew. My nose wrinkled up at the smell of fish and mud. There were other pots simmering on the stove so I figured that they couldn't all be catfish. My adventurous little heart went for the lid on the second pot. I must have hollered pretty loud..."MawMaw is cooking rats!"

My Mama was the first to hot foot it into that kitchen. I had one hand clamped over my mouth and the other one grabbing that pot lid out of my hand. She pushed it back down on the pot and then whispered sternly in my ear, "I told you not to look in those pots. That ain't a rat...it's a squir-rel. MawMaw knows that not everybody likes catfish so she made a few other things to eat."   I will never forget the look of that critter lying in there completely whole but skinned, surrounded by broth and carrots and potatoes. I had a vegetable meal that evening. Later in life, however, I came to like most of the 'strange' meals that my MawMaw made. I have never been overly picky, so I am of the thought that I will try anything once... and in that philosophy, there may have been the very reason that MawMaw always made sure I got first pick at what she made.

My MawMaw was a firm believer in waste not, want not. She made use of anything that could be cooked and eaten. My uncles and cousins were all hunters and MawMaw was the one who got the privilege of cook-ing what was hunted. Going to her house was always an adventure of sorts because you never knew what you were going to find in freezers, cellars, or any other food storage area. I remember hearing my uncle talking to her about three big ol' coons he had 'gotten' earlier. As I have said before, I was the nosy young'un in the family, so I decided I needed to see these big ol' coons....so I went into the kitchen corner where MawMaw's big freezer was and opened the lid. As soon as I looked in, I was greeted by three big raccoons, all baring teeth and claws extended....frozen solid. It was in this moment that I decided that maybe I wasn't the grandchild that MawMaw needed to teach all of her secrets to.

MawMaw had a different idea. My uncle Frank loved possum. I have no idea why, but he did. My Pop's side of the family were simple folks. They ate what they had access to, and a lot of that food was found in nearby woods and whatever may have wandered onto their farms. I can remember like it was yesterday. I had gone to visit MawMaw one Saturday, and when I got there, her first words were, "Oh good. Today you can learn how to cook it." I knew I was in trouble right then. I had no idea what 'it' was but I knew it couldn't be good and that it was probably something that I wouldn't want to touch or taste.

I was right. I looked on the kitchen counter and MawMaw had a whole possum laying there on a piece of newspaper. I looked at that poor critter lying there, and my fear of rats screamed at the top of its lungs. I am trying not to react but all I can see is a giant skint rat lying on that countertop. One thing you have to know about MawMaw is that you never said no to her. She was the matriarch of the family, and she knew it and took it very seriously. It was her job to pass on the traditions of our kin...even if nobody wanted to learn. She looked at me in my state of panic and told me to pull the roaster out from under the cabinet.

As I pulled out the roaster that had held many a turkey or chicken for every major holiday...all I could think of now was the fact that we were about to plop a huge old greasy possum in that roaster, and now everything made in it going forward was going to be warped by the smell and taste of possum.

My uncle Frank would always bring MawMaw the possum that he had 'caught', and she would clean it out for two weeks before cooking it. She would feed it milk and corn (especially since possums will eat anything... especially bugs). My thought, though, was, why worry about that...you are already eating something that, in my humble opinion, should be left alone and let be. Once she had it fattened up and cleaned out, she would boil it and scrape the hair off (this part was done before I got there, thankfully).

Apparently, she had saved the 'easy' stuff for me to help with. As I stand there crippled by fear at the sight of this giant rat, she picks it up and hands it to me, and tells me to hold it while she stuffs it. I remember just trying to imagine myself doing anything else and watching as she pushed potatoes, carrots, and onions into the belly of the beast. She then tells me to carefully put it in the roaster so that the innards don't fall out. I watched with my mouth gaped open as she pries the mouth open and delicately pops a persimmon into the jaws.

Once this traumatic ordeal is over and the possum is in the oven, she invites me into the living room to relax on her bright orange naugahyde sofa. I will never forget the smell that completely enveloped the house... it wasn't unpleasant, but it wasn't a good one either. Of course, MawMaw would look over and every so often exclaim, "Don't that just smell so good? Makes your mouth water, I bet." Well...no. Maybe if I hadn't had to experience the whole process and then getting to look the critter in the eyes once it was out of the oven.

Even in the midst of the shock and completely unexpected, I treasure the wisdom that was shared with me, and I don't take it for granted. Will I use all of these nuggets? Probably not, but I know that I have a piece of family history wedged deep inside that many of my cousins and my brother didn't get to experience. She taught me a deep respect for nature even when she was cooking it.

MawMaw wasn't a rich woman. She made do with what she had. She raised three children by herself and was always there for family. As long as she was alive, nobody was going to do without. When we visited, we were always sent home with bags of potatoes, beans, peas...anything that she grew in her garden. We always tried to help her. Family was important to her and to this day, that legacy has filtered down to all the grandkids and cousins. We all keep up with each other, encourage each other, and make sure that we all have what we need...even it if it just an ear.

I have always heard that when the head of the family is gone, the family dynamic shifts, and the family members move away from the things they were taught. I don't find that to be the case with this side of the family. We still make an effort to talk and check on each other. We tell stories about what all we found in those pots we were warned not to look in, and we can hear MawMaw laughing as we recount those memories. There were times we all wondered if we got to experience what we did just to amuse an old granny who embraced the unusual and quirky parts of her heritage.

As I get older, I see bits of her in me. I love to tell the stories she used to tell me to the young'uns. I love watching their reactions as I tell them some of the things their great great granny did and said and then to see them giggle just from the sheer strangeness of some of these antics. MawMaw had her share of heartaches, disappointments, and pain, but she lived her life in the moment. She knew that those things were all temporal, but that you got out of life what you put into it. She chose a world of laughter and singing as opposed to anger and resentment.

Her life was her family and she lived that life as fully as she knew how. She spoiled her grandkids and made sure that they never left her house feeling hungry or unloved. As I write this, I can hear her in the back of my mind telling me to sing her a song but I also can see her smiling and rocking back and forth in her chair with her eyes closed as I sang.

We forget sometimes that magick isn't always sparks and grand rituals. Sometimes it is as simple as a memory or a song meandering through our soul. The moments I spent with MawMaw were awash with laughter and music and those insignificant everyday moments. It was in those supposedly insignificant moments that I learned what true magick was. MawMaw did everything with passion and intent…everything.

I learned well from her. As I get older and move more and more into my sage years, I will be that uncle/cousin/friend who will try my best to make you laugh and try to show you the magick that exists in those small day to day pieces of life. I want to be like MawMaw…I want to inspire you to dream, to experience life, and to walk in the magick that you may not be able to see on your own.

Life is hard enough. MawMaw came up in hard times. She lived through the depression, wars, the death of family...but she always had a smile, a laugh, or a story to share with anyone who she felt needed it. Was she an eternal optimist? No...but she did believe that if you kept a song in your heart, a story on your lips, and a dash of magick up your sleeve that you could conquer anything.

I still believe every bit of this. MawMaw believed that happiness was temporal but that joy was always a choice. I am learning every day to choose joy. In this day and age when life seems to be so much harder...just surviving takes effort. My goal each morning is to find something that will inspire a heartfelt, gut-wrenching belly laugh. Most of the time, I can find this in myself. When I have a harder time finding something, I always go back to some of the encounters and misadventures I had with MawMaw. I guarantee that wherever she is now, she is laughing and dancing and stirring up some kind of ruckus along with every other member of my family who are now beyond the veil.

Several years ago, I wrote a small daily ritual to help me see and experience the joys in the small everyday happenings. It helps me to be able to have a taste of what MawMaw lived every minute of her life:

Exercise: "Rekindle Your Joy

Objective: This exercise is designed to help you reconnect with the sources of joy in your life, cultivate a positive mindset, and infuse more happiness into your daily routines.

Materials Needed:
- Journal or notebook
- Pen or pencil
- Quiet, reflective space

Instructions:
1. Create a Joy Journal:

Start by dedicating a journal or a section of your existing journal specifically to this exercise. This will be your "Joy Journal" where you document your journey to rekindling joy.

2. Reflect on Past Joyful Moments:

Take a moment to reflect on the moments in your life when you felt truly joyful. These could be recent experiences or memories from your past. Write down at least three of these moments in your Joy Journal.

3. Identify Current Sources of Joy:

List things, activities, or people in your life that currently bring you joy. It could be something as simple as a hobby, a pet, a friend, or a favorite place. Aim to identify at least five sources of joy.

4. Daily Joyful Moments:

Commit to finding and acknowledging at least one joyful moment in your day. It could be a beautiful sunrise, a kind gesture from someone, or a small accomplishment. Write down this daily joyful moment in your Joy

Journal.

5. Gratitude Practice:
Each day, write down three things you are grateful for in your Joy Journal. Gratitude is closely linked to joy, and this practice can help you shift your focus toward positive aspects of your life.

6. Mindful Joy:
Practice mindfulness by fully engaging in activities that bring you joy. Whether it's savoring a favorite meal, going for a nature walk, or playing a musical instrument, be fully present in the moment.

7. Spread Joy to Others:
Identify ways to bring joy to others. Acts of kindness, thoughtful gestures, or simply sharing your positive energy can create a ripple effect of joy. Document these actions in your Joy Journal.

8. Create a Joyful Vision Board:
Gather images, quotes, and symbols that represent joy to you. Create a vision board in your Joy Journal, reminding you of what brings you happiness and inspiration.

9. Challenge Negative Thoughts:
Whenever negative thoughts or self-doubt arise, challenge them by writing down a more positive and realistic perspective in your Joy Journal. Practice self-compassion and self-kindness.

10. Reflect and Adjust:
Periodically review your Joy Journal to track your progress. Celebrate the moments of joy you've documented, and make adjustments to your daily routines to prioritize joy.

11. **Share Your Joy Journey:**

Consider sharing your journey to rekindle joy with a close friend or loved one. Sharing experiences and insights can deepen your connection and create shared moments of happiness.

Let's Do the Working:

Ritual to Rekindle Your Joy

Materials Needed:
   – A small candle (color of your choice, preferably yellow or orange)
   – A lighter or matches
   – A small piece of paper or a sticky note
   – A pen or marker

Ritual Steps:

1. Preparation: Find a quiet and comfortable space where you won't be disturbed. Place the candle, lighter or matches, paper, and pen in front of you.

2. Candle Setting: You can inscribe a symbol onto the candle. It can be as simple or elaborate as you want it to be. It just needs to be something that makes joy take the primary focus. It can even be as simple as carving a smiley face into the candle. Light the candle, focusing on the flame. Visualize the warm and positive energy of the flame representing joy. Take a few deep breaths and let go of any stress or worries.

3. Write Your Spell: On the piece of paper, write a simple spell to invoke joy in your daily life. For example: "In every moment, big or small, let

joy be my guide, let joy be my call." Let this be your call to the universe/ spirits for joy to overtake you in the most ordinary moments of the day. As an example, I have included the spell that I wrote for my own daily ritual:

By moonlight's glow and sun's embrace,
I seek joy in every place.
In moments small and moments grand,
I summon joy with open hands.

With every breath, with every sigh,
May the joy within me never shy.
In laughter, smiles, and simple things,
Let happiness take flight with wings.

With this intent, I speak my spell,
May joy within my heart now dwell.
So shall it be, the magick's spun,
In the small everyday moments, joy has won.

4. Recite the Spell: Hold the paper in your hands and recite the spell you've written. Say it with intention and belief in its power. As you do so, imagine yourself surrounded by a radiant, joyful light.

5. Manifest That Joy: Take a moment to reflect on the small things that bring you joy. It could be the taste of your favorite food, the laughter of a loved one, or the beauty of nature. Feel these moments of joy as if they are happening right now.

6. Charging the Paper: Hold the paper near the candle flame (but not too close to avoid burning it) and visualize the joy you seek infusing into the paper. Imagine the energy of the flame transferring joy to the paper.

7. Express Gratitude: Give thanks for the joy that already exists in your life. Feel gratitude for the small moments of happiness you've experienced.

8. Release the Spell: Gently blow out the candle, imagining that as the flame is extinguished, your intention is released into the universe. Place the paper in a safe and meaningful spot, such as under your pillow or on your altar.

9. Daily Reminders: Each day, when you encounter a small joyful moment, take a moment to recall the spell and the intention you set. This will help reinforce your focus on finding joy in the everyday.

Remember, the power of the ritual comes from your intention, belief, and willingness to engage in the practice. Approach it with an open heart and a positive attitude, and you may find that you're more attuned to experiencing joy in the small moments of your life.

CHAPTER THREE
THE BOOGER WOODS
AND MORE

"Life in itself is a story, where dreams and reality intertwine. We are the heroes, navigating through enchanted forests, facing mythical creatures, and unlocking the secrets of our own hearts. We are the creators of our own extraordinary story."

MawMaw was always the one who walked her own path. She didn't care what anyone thought about her, and I got much of that same nature. She was always the one teaching me how to do things the old fashioned way or instilling a strong belief in all things magickal. She believed that the world was too overtaken by troubles and sadness and that we needed magick in our lives to counter all of that. She would tell me stories of her childhood and kin, and she loved to enthrall me with tales of the Booger Woods and the headless hog. I hope you enjoy it as much as I did:

Not far from where MawMaw grew up, there was a piece of wooded property that was apparently some of the devil's own stomping grounds. We would beg MawMaw to tell us the stories of the Booger Woods. Her eyes would light up and a long drawn-out cackle would spring forth from her:

Well, darlin', gather 'round and let me tell y'all a tale 'bout them Booger Woods down yonder close to the old home place. Now, the Booger Woods, they ain't no place for the faint of heart, 'cause they're full of spooks and spirits, or so folks always said.

Now Bobby, he was a curious feller, always wantin' to see what's what. One hot summer evening, when the sun was settin' low, he decided he wanted to go where few dared to tread – them Booger Woods.

Now, they call 'em Booger Woods for a reason, 'cause the noises that come from there ain't nothin' natural. Sounds like a banshee's wail mixin' with a hootin' owl and a lonesome coyote. Bobby, though, he was made of sterner stuff, or so he thought.

As he stepped deeper into them woods, the trees seemed to close in on him, the dead branches of those trees danglin' like ghosts. The air turned thick with the scent of damp earth, and the night's chill crept up his spine.

That's when Bobby heard it, a guttural, mournful howl that froze his bones. His eyes widened, and he tried to make his way back home, but that's when he saw it – a headless hog, its fur all matted and its eyes a-glowin' with an eerie light(as young'uns we never questioned why a hog with no head had glowing eyes). It moved like it was bein' led by some force he couldn't see.

Bobby's heart started poundin', and he took off like a scared rabbit, the hooves of that headless hog poundin' right behind him. It was a race against the devil, as Bobby put it, and he wasn't sure he'd win.

He burst out of them Booger Woods, his breath ragged, and ran as hard as his feet would carry him to his daddy's old farmhouse. He knew he'd seen somethin' outta this world, somethin' that sent shivers up his spine.

From that day on, Bobby never went near them Booger Woods again. He learned that some things are better left alone, and some stories are better off whispered on a dark summer's night as a warning to the young'uns, and them Booger Woods hold secrets that ain't meant for the livin' to uncover.

I tried my dangedest to get her to show me where those woods were, but she never would. She told me that it wouldn't be on her head if I got eaten by a headless hog....of course, me being the smart ass that I was asked her how it would eat me if it didn't have a head...and oh the look I got from her.

MawMaw knew that I was a skittish kid, but that didn't keep her from enthralling me with her tales of growing up and the off-the-wall and unusual encounters she had. She would often tell me stories of our kin and their misadventures. My grandpa committed suicide before I was born, and most of his family history came from MawMaw or from his living brothers and sisters.

MawMaw was also a superstitious soul. I recall many a story about 'haints' being recounted in many a supper table conversation. As I said before, MawMaw lived downhill from a cemetery...not just any old cemetery, but one specifically for Civil War soldiers and slaves. One of her favorite things to do (and as kids, we were completely enthralled...or as us southerners would say, we ate it up) was to sit in the living room or the at the dining room table, and she would tell us stories of her and other family members encounters with haints. A haint, as defined by Wikipedia: "The word haint is an alternative spelling of haunt, which was historically used in African-American vernacular to refer to a ghost or, in the Hoodoo belief, a witch-like creature seeking to chase victims to their death by exhaustion.[4][5]" Because of the area we lived in and the close proximity to the Gullah peoples, my family used this word interchangeably with ghosts. We grew up with 'haint' being the term of choice used by MawMaw and her side of the family. Even as far away from the Gullah people as her family was, there were still many of the old family houses with the ceiling of the front porch painted 'haint blue' to ward off those particular beings. Not having grown up in the Hoodoo tradition or trained in it, the term was a broader term for ghosts and malevolent spirits.

I remember many a warning as we would wander around that old cemetery..."Don't be bringing no haints back up in here. I worked hard to keep this house safe and clean. Looking back, there was always a pot of something simmering on the stove to 'clear the air.' The distinct smell of rosemary and a few other protective herbs were common aromas wafting through the air. MawMaw also believed in leaving windows and doors open and sweeping that air around to keep it moving.

When I think back to so many of those things I just saw as normal daily activities, now I recognize the use of them in my own daily practices. The stories and traditions that MawMaw passed down are still so much a part of my life…and all the nephews and nieces love to sit on my lap and listen to the stories that were passed down. There is still nothing better than settling in with a hot cup of coffee, a piece of cold oven pound cake, and a story that brings just as much excitement and an outcrop of goosebumps to pass a slow southern evening.

A part of MawMaw's stories were also based in the superstitions she held. I remember Mama telling me about how, when her and Pop lived with MawMaw after they first got married, Ma would sit in front of the television watching wildlife shows. When she would see a snake onscreen, my mama, just in silliness, would flick her tongue out like a snake. This got MawMaw all riled up and she would put her hand on her hip and say, "If you keep doing that, you are going to mark that baby." Ma didn't think anything about it and when I was born, I was lying in the cradle one day and, based on what Ma told me, I stuck my tongue out and pushed it up to touch my nose. MawMaw yelled, "Pat, get in here! See?! This is what I was talking about….you done marked that young'un." I don't think I ever figured out just what being 'marked' did for me or to me, but I have never been afraid of snakes, have had many an encounter with them, but based on the way MawMaw reacted to it, it must have been something that wasn't sought after.

MawMaw wasn't the only storyteller, though. Ma's mom, (we called her Nannie), was another that liked to tell stories. When her and her sisters and brothers would get together, it was a virtual story hour. They always started with the ones that would give the kids nightmares…but then again, we would always sneak into the corners of the rooms to listen, even when we knew the adults were 'visiting.'

Nannie would always reminisce with her sisters about the birth and death of her first daughter, Barbara Ann. Barbara was a healthy baby when she was born, but back in those days, infant mortality was a big concern and the diseases that were out there and no vaccines or vaccines still being created for them was a big part of life. The story of Barbara was a sweet one but haunting and devastating at the same time.

Nannie always told the story starting out with what a quiet and calm baby Barbara was. Never fussed...never cried much at all. She was born in January 1940. It was in April of that same year that Nannie and her sisters were standing around the kitchen talking and exchanging stories, as was typical of their family get-togethers.

As the women were all circled up in the corner, having coffee and poundcake, my aunt Ruby Jean saw a pink rose appear in the upper corner of the kitchen above the stove. It floated from that corner of the room and moved clockwise along the perimeter, and it stopped just above the bassinet where Barbara was asleep. Apparently, for that side of the family, this was something that had happened before and was to be taken seriously. All of the women rallied around Nannie, knowing what was now looming.

It was less than a week later that Barbara came down with bacterial meningitis and passed away quietly in her sleep. Infant mortality was something that most families had to deal with in those days, and I can't imagine the pain of losing a child, but I also know that, in my family, in particular, this was a way to keep the memories of those who passed beyond the veil, close. Whenever Nannie, or any other member of the family talked about Barbara (or any other family members who had passed away), they were talked about as if they were very much alive...very much a part of the family and someone who held a place in our hearts.

The women in our family weren't the only ones with stories to share. There were many days that I sat in the living room at Nannie and Paw-

Paw's house and listened intently as PawPaw would tell stories of his time spent in the army. He was stationed all over, and I can remember the tales of wartime and how he managed to keep his sanity in the midst of turmoil.

He would tell me of the buddies he made in the military and how those men had become family...even brothers to him. It was through these stories that I found the gumption to take whatever life threw at me and try to make the best of the situation or circumstances. As PawPaw talked about the pranks and stories and laughs that he and his buddies shared just to be able to come through a horrifying part of history like war, it taught me that we, as a people, can be as resilient and as strong as we are required to be in a particular timeframe.

It was through the stories of a war-torn world and the suffering that I learned a bit about strength and perserverence. We have to see these pieces of history...not so that they can be glorified, but so that they aren't repeated. I know that PawPaw altered the stories for the benefit of young ears, but even in those modifications, the spirit of a group of soldiers shown through. It is because of his stories that I have learned to accept people, no matter their background or belief system, and I have forged my own support system made up of many people who don't practice magick the way I do. Friendship isn't about the differences...even though they can be beneficial in the growth of the spirit, but about finding the common ground with which to embrace those who don't look, sound, act, or believe the way that we do.

It was through the stories shared by my grandparents and family members that I came to understand that movement of the physical to the spirit was a very natural transition and that it didn't mean that those loved ones were no longer with us, but they were still a large part of our lives and that we still have access to them and their wisdom. It was also through the sharing of these stories that I learned who I was and where I came from. I come from survivors and fighters and those willing to accept the trauma that life brings but are willing to put in the work to overcome the challenges presented to them.

Exercise: "Honoring and Sharing Family Stories"

Objective: This exercise is designed to help you connect with your family's or ancestral heritage, preserve cherished stories, and share them with future generations.

Materials Needed:
  – Journal or notebook
  – Pen or pencil
  – Access to family members or ancestral information (photos, documents, etc.)

Instructions:
  1. Create a Family Heritage Journal:
      Start by dedicating a journal or a section of your existing journal as your "Family Heritage Journal." This will be your space to collect and record stories and information about your family or ancestors.

  2. Research Your Family History:
      Begin by gathering as much information as you can about your family tree. Talk to older family members, consult family documents, or use genealogy websites to trace your lineage. Record names, dates, and places.

  3. Interview Family Members:
      Reach out to family members, especially elders, and conduct interviews to capture their personal stories, memories, and experiences. Ask open-ended questions about their upbringing, traditions, and significant

life events.

4. Collect Family Photos and Memorabilia:

Gather old family photos, letters, recipes, and any other memorabilia that hold sentimental value. These items can provide valuable insights and visuals to accompany your family stories.

5. Document Ancestral Stories:

Write down the stories and anecdotes you've gathered, focusing on those that capture the essence of your family's heritage. Include details like names, dates, locations, and the emotional significance of each story.

6. Create a Family Tree:

Draw or create a family tree to visually represent your lineage. Include names, birthdates, and any other relevant information you've collected. This can serve as a reference point for your family's history.

7. Reflect on Shared Values and Traditions:

Explore the values, traditions, and cultural aspects that have been passed down through your family. Write about how these have shaped your identity and the values you hold dear.

8. Write Personal Reflections:

Share your own reflections on what you've learned about your family or ancestors. Discuss how these stories have influenced your life and your connection to your heritage.

9. Digitize and Organize:

Consider digitizing family photos and documents to ensure their preservation. Organize these files systematically, creating a digital archive for future generations.

10. Share Stories with Family:

Plan a family gathering or virtual meeting to share the collected stories and family tree with relatives. Encourage them to contribute their own stories and memories.

11. Create a Family Heritage Book:

If you wish, compile the stories, photos, and family tree into a printed or digital family heritage book. This can be a treasured keepsake for your family.

12. Pass It On:

Encourage younger family members to continue this tradition by involving them in the process and teaching them about their heritage. Emphasize the importance of passing down family stories.

Let's Do the Work:

Ritual for Honoring and Sharing Family Stories

Materials Needed:
- A comfortable and quiet space
- An item that represents the stories that have been passed down
- A candle and matches or a lighter
- A journal or notebook
- Optional: A family recipe, an heirloom, or any relevant objects

Steps:
1. Set the Space: Find a calm and peaceful space where you won't be disturbed. Set up a comfortable area with a cushion or chair.

2. Candle Lighting: Light the candle as a symbol of illumination and connection. Take a few deep breaths to center yourself and create a tranquil atmosphere.

3. Reflect on the Stories: Hold the item that represents the family stories you hold close to your heart. Close your eyes and take a moment to reflect on those stories. Visualize the faces of your kin, their stories, and their experiences.

4. Invoke Your Kin: Speak aloud or silently address your kinfolk, inviting their presence into the ritual. Express gratitude for the wisdom and stories they've passed down through the generations.

5. Share Those Memories: If you have family members present, invite them to share a cherished family story or memory. If you're alone, reflect on a story that has been passed down to you.

6. Write in your Journal: Take your journal and begin to write down the story or memory that was shared. Add any details, emotions, or insights that come to mind. This is a way to honor and preserve these stories for future generations.

7. Connect with the Objects: If you have family recipes, heirlooms, or objects that carry significance, take a moment to hold them. Reflect on the hands that held these items before you and the stories they hold.

8. Express Gratitude: Take a moment to express your gratitude to your kinfolk for their legacy. Speak from the heart or silently in your thoughts, thanking them for the stories that shape who you have become.

9. Candle Dedication: Hold your hands over the lit candle (a safe distance away), visualizing the flame as a conduit between you and your kinfolk. Offer a few words of dedication, expressing your intention to carry forward their stories and honor their lives.

10. Close the Ritual: Blow out the candle, symbolizing the completion of the ritual. Know that the connections and insights you've gained during this ritual will remain with you.

11. Continue the Tradition: Consider making this ritual a regular practice to honor your family's stories and keep the connections alive. You can also share these stories with younger family members, ensuring that the wisdom of your ancestors is passed down to future generations. I often will sit down with my nephews and niece in my lap when I visit home and tell them the stories that MawMaw, PawPaw, and Nannie told me. I watch their eyes light up with amazement as they listen and ask questions.

This ritual is a personal and meaningful way to connect with your family's history. Adapt it to fit your beliefs and feelings, and let the stories flow through you as you honor the stories passed from generation to generation.

CHAPTER FOUR
MY WILD, UNRULY KIN

"My wild unruly ancestor, a rebel spirit in the past,
Your untamed legacy, through time, forever lasts.
A force of nature, unbound and free,
Your essence echoes now, through me."

It's funny, in a way, the way that we all tend to put our ancestors in a box. We have these grand thoughts of being descended from royalty, or, in the South, everyone seems to have a Cherokee princess in their family tree (or so they were told). Over the past couple of decades, I have been researching my family tree. I have gotten some amazing information and have been able to trace my heritage back to Scotland, Ireland, and England. I have gone through boxes and boxes of photographs, letters, and documents in my search, and I can honestly say I haven't been disappointed.

Is there royalty? Not really, but I have found many Lairds and Ladies in my family tree. Have I found land moguls? No, but I have found many farmers and sharecroppers and folks who made their living off the land. Have I found celebrities and famous people? No, but I have found characters with strong personalities who lived their lives without apology and without compromise.

One of my family members who has made her way to the top of the family tree is my great great granny, Thula Pigg. Thula was a strong presence in my family and was known for her unorthodox lifestyle choices. Thula was born in Union County, North Carolina, in 1875 to John Wesley and Mary Helton Pigg. Looking at her photo, you would imagine she was a simple country woman with no skeletons in her closet.

Well, Thula was neither simple nor without her skeletons. Thula was the mother of a brood of her own and unmarried. According to stories from my dad, she was a stubborn woman who didn't feel that being tied to one man held much credence. Thula had six children, and rumor has it that they each had a different daddy. She kept her maiden name and didn't believe, as other women of the time did, that marriage made an honest woman out of you.

My great great grandpa was a Hildreth, but the son they had together was given his mother's last name and passed that name down to his children. Piggs and Hildreths are intermingled through that whole part of family history, so it isn't such a far-fetched idea that there may have been tangled relations throughout that whole side of the family.

Thula was tough. She didn't care what other people thought of her and she marched to her own drum. She was independent and willing to do whatever it took to take care of her little herd. As I listened to the stories, I could feel her independent nature and her strength flowing through the words. Pop has always been a bit reserved, so to hear him tell stories about his wanton grandmother was comical to say the least.

I teach a class on meeting your ancestors where you are and I like to refer to great great granny Thula as the family Wildcard. I love the fact that this powerful, uninhibited woman is a part of me. I call to her spirit often in my workings just because I am an introvert by nature, and it is her spirit that supplies wisdom and power and an uninhibited way of looking at things. She is the one I call to when I need an extra dose of 'gumption.'

For those of you who may not have grown up using the word 'gumption,' it is a word that many Southerners adopted from our Scottish ancestry. At first, gumption had a simple meaning...to have common sense. Over the years, it has also come to encompass courage, get up and go, or, as would be said in Yiddish, chutzpah. It has also evolved to embrace qualities like wisdom, wit, and street smarts. Thula embraced all of those attributes wholeheartedly and within me is that same grit and fortitude.

I have found, as I get older, that more and more of Thula comes out. I find it harder to tolerate judgmental and hateful ways of thinking or the thought that people need to fit neatly into a box or package. Folks are as different as leaves or snowflakes and should be cherished for those reasons alone. I refuse to expect someone to conform to my thoughts of how they should be. People flourish when you stop putting limits on them. This was something that great great granny Thula lived every day of her life...a life without the limits that others impose.

Not everyone in the family tree can be a force like Thula, but each one holds their own place and significance in the history of my family. One of those family members is my uncle Zeb. He was my grandpa's youngest brother.According to family members, Zeb was a quiet soul...even as a youngster. He was said to have the *second sight*. This isn't something new to my family. Many of us have been gifted with this and have navigated our way through learning how to use it without it becoming the chain that it became for Zeb. From what I have been told, I look very much like my uncle Zeb, but I have also been told that I was the spitting image of my grandpa Wid when he was younger. I have a few photos of my grandpa but only one of a young well-groomed uncle Zeb. It was said that he lived his life in overalls and did his best to deal with the voices that seemed to plague him. He avoided hospitals, funerals, cemeteries...all of the places where the voices seemed to call the loudest.

MawMaw told me that he was 34 when he decided to silence those voices. Most folks today would say that maybe he was dealing with schizophrenia or mental issues, but the family would tell you that he was completely normal and a gentle soul...he just needed to learn how to keep the voices quiet at times. Uncle Zeb found an old milk crate and sat on the railroad track until the train rumbled over the tracks and silenced those voices for him once and for all.

In my own ancestral workings, I find it intriguing that Zeb seems to be the most vocal. I have seen him in dreams and in visions, and he can talk your ear off. I guess that when he moved past the veil, that things became clearer for him and a lot less scary. He still presents a gentle spirit and one who has been willing to teach me how to work with and direct that heirloom of a gift that he passed down to me.

Zeb has the heart of a teacher beyond the veil. I remember my first encounter with him and how he meekly engaged me in a dream. He was standing by my bed, and I heard him clear his throat. I recognized him from the photo, but he introduced himself with dignity and kindness. "Hey there. I'm your uncle Zeb. Been watching out for you for some time now and figured it was time we got to know each other." I can remember every part of that dream so vividly. He led me to a porch with a couple of rocking chairs. In hindsight, I recognize the house as the old homeplace. My aunt Ruby inherited the house and land when her mama and daddy died and now it is one of those modern two-story houses with little to no yard. Before, it was a beautiful old farmhouse with a wrap-around porch and lots of farmland.

As we settled into the rockers and watched the lightning bugs flicker in the distance, Zeb told me stories of what 'the sight' was like for him. The constant bombardment of voices and ethereal noises. He admitted that if he had taken the time to learn to tune them out when needed or at least tell them to honor his mental space, that he might have been around to meet me in person. He explained in his quiet and gentle way how I had been gifted with the sight and that it was time to take ownership. He knew that as a young'un and teenager that I had completely shut down this 'gift' out of fear of ending up like he did. As a kid, I steered clear of all the places he had avoided…no funerals, and no hospitals.. I find it funny sometimes when I think back to my years as a pastor…I spent nearly every day in one or more of those places. Again, I had become particularly adept at shutting down this part of my senses and walked through the process rather mechanically. The living I interacted with were never short-changed when it came to empathy, sympathy, or caring, but the dead were left to fend for themselves whenever I was around. Zeb has taught me how to offer the same caring and genuine empathy for those who have crossed the veil and need direction or just someone to talk to.

Many of my ancestors were bigger than life when they were alive. As a very backward and introverted child, I didn't quite know what to do with them when I was around them. Pop's side of the family always kept me on my guard and even scared me just a bit. MawMaw's sisters were all characters in their own right. When they laughed, it wasn't a chuckle or a giggle…it was a full-on screech. My aunt Christine was such a gentle and loving woman, but a five-year-old doesn't quite know what to do with a large woman who unhinged her jaw and let out a blood-curdling scream that sounded like a mix of hyena and excruciating pain. As an adult, I had learned to appreciate her full abandon and larger than life personality. I think back on it and now realize that those sisters all embraced life and grabbed it by the balls. They were completely unfazed by the opinions of anyone else, and thankfully, a part of that was passed down to me.

My uncle Frank…the brother of my grandpa Wid and uncle Zeb was another one who scared me to death as a young'un. I remember him as rough as a cob and always in overalls. He walked with his head tilted to the left side due to a combination of vertigo and hearing loss and with a limp which added to my fear. I don't think he really knew much about how to relate to kids because his one go-to phrase when we would go visit was, "You want me to cut off your ear?" Of course, that would send me running back to the car as fast as my stubby little legs could go, and then Pop would come over and try to calm me down. "He's only kidding. Saying stuff like that is how he likes to have fun." Yeah…fun. I would sit in the living room perched on the edge of a chair or sofa planning my escape just in case I ever saw a pocket knife come out. I came to realize as I got older that he was harmless and not very socially adept. He had lived all of his life on a farm, and the only folks he interacted with were his wife and daughters. As he aged, our visits were spent talking about weather, animals, family, and, of course, his love of eating possum.

I have come to understand, as I work with and research my ancestry, that people come in all sorts of wrappings. I can glean experiences and understanding from each one if I take the time and set my intention. In my family tree, there are many personalities, some wild and strange…but that's ok. I can learn something from all of them, even when they have or do scare me to death. I have learned through my ancestor work that if I approach each one with respect and a genuine desire to get to know them (the person and the spirit), that I can access all of the magick that they hold. They are part of me. I am part of them. As we partner together in magick, there is healing, understanding, and strength. I am the culmination of centuries of magick and am who I am because of my kin.

I find it a bit humorous that at some point I will take my place alongside my wild, unruly ancestors. I will be the one who is called on. I will be that one wild card. The legacy of magick that I will be able to pass down will live on through those who come after me and they will be able to say that is my weird uncle…just put an offering of cake on the altar and he's good.

Ancestral magick holds great importance to me due to its deep connection with my heritage and lineage. Ancestral magick itself refers to the magickal practices, wisdom, and energy passed down through generations within a family or community. Here are a few reasons why ancestral magick is considered important:

A. Cultural Identity: Ancestral magick helps me to connect with my own cultural roots, preserving and honoring family traditions, rituals, and spiritual beliefs. It serves as a way to maintain a sense of identity and heritage.

B. Wisdom and Knowledge: Ancestors possess accumulated knowledge and wisdom from their experiences. Ancestral magick allows me to tap into this wisdom, gaining insights, guidance, and teachings that have been passed down for generations.

C.   Spiritual Connection: Ancestors are often regarded as spiritual guides or protectors. Engaging with ancestral magick helps to deepen my own spiritual connection, and fosters a sense of belonging and support from the spiritual realm.

D.   Healing and Transformation: Ancestral magick has offered a path for my own healing from ancestral wounds and traumas. By acknowledging and working with ancestral energy, I have been able to address unresolved issues, find closure, and experience personal transformation.

E.   Intergenerational Bonding: Practicing ancestral magick has helped me to foster a connection between generations, has helped to strengthen family ties, and has promoted intergenerational learning. It has provided opportunities for me to share stories, rituals, and customs and to create an ongoing sense of unity and continuity within my own practices and within my immediate family.

It's important to note that the significance of ancestral magick varies across cultures and individuals, but overall, it serves as a means of honoring the past, seeking guidance, and embracing one's cultural heritage. There are cultures who don't engage or work with the spirits of the dead, so look at the history and practices within your own heritage before delving into working with the spirits of those who have moved beyond the veil.

Part of my own practice has involved creating sacred space for my ancestors and allowing them a place in my own journey and craft. I have created an Ancestral altar using the principles and practices below:

Setting up a sacred space for ancestral magick can create a dedicated and energetically supportive environment for connecting with your ancestors. Here are some steps that I have used to help to establish a sacred space for ancestral magick:

A. Choose a Location: Select a quiet and comfortable space in your home where you can set up your sacred area. It could be a corner of a room, a shelf, a table, or any space that feels meaningful to you.

B. Cleanse and Purify the Space: Before setting up your sacred space, cleanse the area energetically. You can do this by burning herbs like rosemary, sage, palo santo, or incense. I use rosemary primarily because of my Scottish ancestry. Saining is the practice of blessing, protecting, or consecrating the space using water and smoke. Traditional herbs used in saining are juniper and rosemary. Clearing the space helps remove any stagnant or unwanted energies.

C. Ancestor Altar or Display: Create an ancestor altar or display as the centerpiece of your sacred space. Place photos, heirlooms, or sentimental objects that remind you of your ancestors. Include items that symbolize their cultural heritage, such as traditional artifacts, family heirlooms, or symbols of their beliefs. I have photos of my great great granny Thula, uncle Zeb, Papa, great aunt Penelope Abigail, and my great grandma Nancy Jane above my altar. I also have a dirt dauber's nest (MawMaw's nickname was Dobby because they said she was shaped like a dirt dauber), and a repurposed hand mirror that belonged to granny Thula. I made it into a scrying mirror with a piece of obsidian.

D. Offerings: Dedicate a space on your altar or nearby for offerings to your ancestors. These offerings can be food, drink, candles, flowers, or other items that were meaningful to your ancestors. Choose offerings based on their cultural background or personal preferences you may know about them. I always make sure to add snuff, pipes, plants, and foods that were favorites of theirs in life.

E. Ritual Tools: Include ritual tools that hold significance to you and your ancestral practices. This could be candles, incense, crystals, divination tools, or any items that resonate with your spiritual connection to your ancestors.

F. Sacred Symbols: Incorporate sacred symbols associated with your ancestral heritage. These symbols can be religious or cultural symbols, ancestral sigils, or representations of your lineage. Place them on or near your altar to honor your ancestral roots. I have a Scottish thistle encased in glass and a Scottish hagstone that I use to connect with those Scottish ancestors I have found in my family tree.

G. Ritual and Meditation Space: Designate a space within your sacred area for meditation, reflection, and ancestral rituals. You can place cushions, a small mat, or a comfortable chair to create a peaceful and inviting space for connecting with your ancestors. I have created a small altar in the woods for this purpose. It seemed like a natural flow considering many of my ancestors were farmers and people who lived off the land.

H. Personalize and Evolve: As you deepen your connection with your ancestors, feel free to personalize and evolve your sacred space. Add or remove items based on your intuition, insights, or new information you discover about your ancestors. The sacred space should reflect your evolving relationship with your ancestral energies.

I. Remember, the most important aspect of creating a sacred space for ancestral magick is the intention and the sincerity you bring to it. Treat this space with reverence, respect, and regular maintenance to honor and nurture your connection with your ancestors.

Exercise: "Ancestral Storytelling"

Objective: This exercise invites you to explore your family's ancestral stories and create a meaningful narrative that connects you to your heritage.

Instructions:
  1. Gather Materials:
     – A quiet and comfortable space.
     – A notebook or computer for recording your thoughts.
     – A favorite family photo or memento if available.
  2. Reflection:

  Begin by taking a few moments to reflect on the idea of ancestral stories. Consider how the stories of your ancestors might have shaped your family's history and traditions.

  3. Family Discussion:

  If possible, engage in a conversation with older family members, such as grandparents, parents, or aunts and uncles. Ask them to share stories about their own parents or grandparents. Encourage them to recount tales of family traditions, significant life events, or memorable experiences from the past.

  4. Journaling:

  Write down the stories and anecdotes shared by your family members. Be sure to capture details, emotions, and any historical context they provide.

  Include your own reflections on how these stories have influenced your family dynamics and values.

  5. Visual Aids:

  If you have a family photo or memento related to the stories you've heard, bring it into your workspace. Use it as a visual aid to connect with the past.

  6. Create Your Ancestral Story:

Now, take all the information you've gathered and craft a narrative that encapsulates the essence of your ancestral stories. Write it as if you were sharing it with someone who knows nothing about your family.

Include details about the challenges your ancestors faced, their triumphs, and the values they held dear. Emphasize the cultural and historical context that influenced their lives.

7. Personal Reflection:

Consider how the ancestral stories you've explored have impacted your own life. Are there values, traditions, or wisdom passed down through generations that resonate with you?

8. Share Your Story:

If you're comfortable, share your newly created ancestral story with your family. Encourage them to add their insights and corrections if needed. This process can strengthen family bonds and create a shared sense of history.

9. Ongoing Connection:

Continue to explore and document ancestral stories as you uncover more. Maintain an ongoing dialogue with family members to keep the tradition of storytelling alive.

Let's Do the Working:

Ritual for Ancestral Magick

Performing a ritual for ancestral magick can be a beautiful and powerful way to honor and connect with your ancestors.

Materials Needed:
– A comfortable and quiet space
– Photos, mementos, symbols, and offerings that represent your ancestors and their cultural heritage

– A candle and matches or a lighter (I use white candles for this ritual)
– A journal or notebook

Preparation:

Cleanse the space: Clear the ritual space of any negative or stagnant energies by smudging, using sacred herbs, or performing a cleansing ritual.

Set up the altar: Create a dedicated altar or sacred space specifically for ancestral magick. Arrange photos, mementos, symbols, and offerings that represent your ancestors and their cultural heritage.

Invocation:

Light a candle or candles on the altar, symbolizing the presence of your ancestors.

Ground yourself and enter a meditative state. Focus your attention on your breath and visualize a connection with your ancestral lineage.

Ancestor Connection:

Call upon your ancestors: Speak a heartfelt invocation, calling upon your ancestors by name or by referring to them as a collective ancestral presence.

Express gratitude: Express gratitude for their presence, guidance, and the wisdom they bring to your life.

Below is an invocation that I wrote for my workings:

Oh, ancestors who came before us,
Whose wisdom and strength we hold dear,
We gather here to honor and remember,
Your presence always near.

With gratitude, we offer our prayer,
For the guidance you bestow,
In times of joy and times of despair,

Your wisdom helps us grow.

May your spirits watch over us,
As we navigate life's path,
Grant us courage, love, and trust,
To face challenges with resolve and grace.

We seek your blessings and protection,
For our family and all who came before,
May your legacy be our inspiration,
Forever cherished, forevermore.

In humble reverence, we bow our heads,
In unity, we honor your name,
May the bond between us never fade,
Our gratitude forever aflame.

To our ancestors, we send this prayer,
With love and reverence, we convey,
Your presence and guidance we hold dear,
Now and for eternity, we shall always pray.

Offerings and Communication:

Offerings: Place offerings on the altar that hold significance to your ancestors, such as food, drinks, flowers, or other items representing their cultural traditions.

Communication and dialogue: Speak to your ancestors, sharing stories, asking for guidance, or expressing any concerns or intentions you have. Listen attentively for any messages, signs, or sensations you may receive in response.

Ritual Actions:

Perform specific rituals or actions associated with your ancestral traditions or beliefs. This could include chanting, singing ancestral songs, reciting prayers, or conducting rituals unique to your ancestral lineage.

If you have specific rituals passed down through your family, honor and incorporate them into the ritual as well.

Closing:

Express gratitude: Thank your ancestors for their presence, guidance, and the blessings they bring to your life.

Extinguish the candle(s) or leave them burning safely, depending on your preference and the duration of the ritual.

Close the ritual space: Conclude the ritual by thanking the spirits, guides, or deities you invoked and express your intention to close the ritual space.

Remember, this is a general framework, and you can customize it based on your specific ancestral practices, cultural traditions, and personal beliefs. Trust your intuition, follow your heart, and create a ritual that feels authentic and meaningful to you and your connection with your ancestors.

CHAPTER FIVE
BREAKING THOSE OLD
FAMILY CURSES

"Magick has the power to mend the broken pieces of the soul, to weave together healing and resilience in the aftermath of trauma. It's not about erasing the past but about transforming it, turning pain into strength, and darkness into light. With the right intention, love, and self-care, the chains of trauma can be broken."

You can probably tell by now that there are a few issues that have been passed down through my family DNA. A few of those 'gifts' that have been shared with the younger generations are Depression, Anxiety, and Suicide. I am a firm believer in addressing family curses with the four M's. Magick, Medication, Mediation, and Meditation. I still have my day-to-day struggles with Anxiety, but thanks to all of the means mentioned above, the other two have remained in check and manageable over a few decades now. Let's take a look at how I have utilized these principles in my own journey through battling and conquering those genealogical 'giftings' that my family has held onto so tightly.

Let's start with how I have used Magick to address the depression and suicidal thoughts that my family so generously passed down. My practice is probably more eclectic and includes Traditional Wytchcraft and Appalachian Folk Magick. Having been raised not far from the Smoky Mountains and having kinfolk scattered all over the mountains and valleys of

North Carolina, I have had the opportunity to enjoy getting to know some of the old granny wytches and their practices.

I have found that in dealing with 'family hand-me-downs' that Ancestor magick is particularly helpful and effective. Like MawMaw used to say, sometimes you've got to get the information straight from the horse's mouth. Looking back at the history in my family…especially with regard to mental health, the men seem to be plagued more than the women. I want to go ahead and address the elephant in the room as we move into this topic. Mental health issues are not 'family secrets.' They are pieces of us that have to be talked about, addressed, and treated. I feel that if my family members who had depression and were suicidal had had the resources we have today, that possibly they would have enjoyed a longer and fuller life.

At an early age, I could feel the fingers of depression and anxiety wrapping methodically around my throat. Even as a little boy, I knew that there was something that kept an overpowering melancholy looming over me. I never understood what this was until years later, when I finally 'broke.' I went to bed one night and stayed there for weeks. I didn't cry, I wasn't angry…I wasn't anything. There was nothing left of me. Ma came into my room one Sunday, and as I lay there wrapped in a smothering blanket of depression and anxiety, she said to me, "You have always been my strong one, my rock. I am watching that rock crumble before my eyes, and I can't do anything about it."

As I watched her move from the side of my bed to the door, I could hear her sniffling, and as she walked away, I felt her hands running through my hair. It was a wake-up call for me. I decided at that point that I had to do something, if not for me but for my family. I called a local psychologist and explained what was happening and made my first appointment. Once I started the counseling sessions, I was able to see that there was something additional needed. I pulled myself up by the bootstraps with every ounce of strength I could muster and I went out behind the house where the chicken coop was, sat under a tree, and poured my heart out to anything and anyone who would listen. I fell asleep under that tree, and in the process, I dreamed about my best friend, who had committed suicide just after we graduated. He was standing in front of me and told me that I couldn't fight this battle by myself and that I needed help from the other side. He told me that he was willing to walk with me and that there were relatives beyond the veil who wanted to walk with me as well.

At this point in my life, I hadn't done much work with ancestral magick, so I was learning as I went. I didn't know much about my ancestors then and didn't know where to start. I started asking Ma and Pop questions about the members of my family who had dealt with depression and suicide. I was amazed by the number of men who had fought the battle with mental health and determined that suicide was their solution. My uncles, cousins, and grandpa were all the subject of many questions that had been left unanswered for years.

I was new to the Craft back then, and like I said, I was learning and had no idea where to start. My starting point was simple and basic. I was sitting under my old tree once again behind the chicken coop, and I opened my mouth, and the only thing that spewed forth was a cry for help. It was one word, but it was the most powerful spell I have ever used. "HELP!" In that moment, I could sense my ancestors rallying around me...enveloping me in a magick that I can't to this day put into words. In looking back, I can now see that each spirit that I work with so closely now was there. I could feel the gently comforting nature of Zeb. There was also the no-nonsense, strong, indomitable spirit of Thula. Papa was there and I could feel the hand of that gentle giant wrapped around my shoulder. There was one there, that I know but have never been able to engage in magick since...my grandpa Wid. His energy was familiar to me. I had felt it many times... especially when my dad was moving things into storage and I touched the gun that he had used to release himself from this life. I plead with these caring and beautiful spirits..."All I am asking is for relief. I need to experience some joy...something besides hurt and pain." It was in that moment that I could feel, for lack of a better phrase, a good swift kick in my back-side. I felt a type of resurgence of my own spirit. I hadn't felt it or wanted to feel it for months. I knew that I was on the right track and started doing the work required to keep this horrible disease at bay.

At first, I relied solely on the counselling and the exercises provided by the psychologist. I was having to reach deep into the parts of myself that I had either hidden or completely shut down. I didn't know it at the time, but it was my first experience with shadow work. I was having to delve into my own heart and psyche and learn how to put pieces together again. I had become my own human jigsaw puzzle. It seemed that there were more missing pieces than answers. I had tried my best to keep my sexual-ity under wraps. When you live in a small town and in the country, it can be dangerous to let folks know that you're gay. I had to be willing to accept myself before anyone else would. I had also buried so much childhood trauma that I didn't want to accept or acknowledge.

I continued my trips to the woods behind the chicken coop and to the pond behind the house. With each trip, I could feel my resolve getting stronger. I could feel my spirit igniting once again. The whole time I was making these little excursions, there was always an animal or two by my side. I feel like the gentle, non-judging spirit that held helped in my heal-ing. It wasn't unusual for me to fall asleep under a tree without waking up with an Australian Shepherd with his or her head in my lap. It was in this communal presence of nature that my healing started. I started noticing that the more time I spent bare-footed and sitting in the grass or wading in the pond that my spirit felt lighter. I learned later that this is actually called grounding, and after seeing the difference it made, I tried my best to do it any chance I got.

It was during this time of self-discovery and magick that I learned how to use my teeth and claws. I found that I was trying way too hard to please everyone and that I needed boundaries. Don't get me wrong, you need to be available for others, and you need to offer encouragement and support, but I was doing this to the detriment of my own heart and spirit. I had forgotten to take care of me. I was essentially walking through life in a stupor...offering what I had to others without refilling and refueling. I can say now that I have learned that I cannot be all things to all people and I am living life as my authentic self.

As I have grown in my magick, I have worked alongside my ancestors to show me where the chinks are in my armor and how to keep myself protected and my magick working at its fullest potential. It took a while, but I have taken on Thula's mantra of "I am who I am." I make no apologies and I stand in the power that I am completely perfect as I am. Yes, I have flaws. Yes, I make mistakes, but as long as I live my life with purpose and stand in my own magick, I can do anything.

My ancestors now have names and faces that I can look to for guidance. They were there even when I didn't know them by name, and they have been faithful. They have shown me that struggles come and go and that as we walk the path of magick that they don't have to become crippling. I have learned to emulate the strengths of each ancestor I work with and to apply what they have to teach me. Zeb has taught me to act in love and gentleness. Thula has taught me to be tough as nails and not let the opinions of others weigh me down. Like the phoenix, we were never meant to burn to ashes and remain. We were born to rise above and to become stronger with each new incarnation of ourselves and our spirits.

Some of the practices I have incorporated in my own path that have helped me to create an atmosphere of healing and respite from past trauma are detailed below:

A. Ancestral healing ceremonies: These are intentional rituals designed to address specific past traumas within my ancestral lineage. These ceremonies aim to bring healing and resolution to unresolved issues that may have been passed down through generations (the depression that hung around my neck like a giant rock). This process, for me, involves creating a sacred space, setting intentions, and using the tools from the previous chapter, such as meditation, visualization, and offerings to connect with and honor my ancestors. By acknowledging and releasing these ancestral traumas, I can help break negative patterns and promote healing within myself and my lineage. It's important to approach such ceremonies and rituals with a deep respect and honor for those you are engaging.

B.   Energy work with ancestors: Utilizing ancestor magick to balance and restore emotional well-being. Energy work with ancestors through ancestor magick involves harnessing the spiritual connections to your ancestors to restore emotional well-being. This is an important piece in drawing on the healing energies and guidance of your ancestors. By tapping into their wisdom and support, you can work to balance and release emotional blockages, finding a sense of healing and renewal.

C.   Working Through Trauma with Ancestor Magick

D.   Transformative storytelling: This is a process that I have personally used. I have always been a huge advocate of 'rewriting our story.' I have used storytelling as a therapeutic tool to reframe and process my own traumatic experiences. Transformative storytelling can be a powerful therapeutic approach. By engaging with traumatic experiences through narratives, I have been able to reframe, process, and gain new perspectives on my own past, which has aided in my own healing and personal growth. It has allowed me to externalize my emotions and thoughts, fostering a deeper understanding of my feelings. This process was initiated by a trained professional and has contributed to the gradual reduction of the emotional impact of my own trauma.

E.   Ancestral spirit guides: Cultivating relationships with ancestral spirits to offer guidance and support during the healing journey. Cultivating relationships with ancestral spirits has been crucial in my own trauma work. I believe that connecting with the spirits of my ancestors has provided guidance, wisdom, and emotional support during my healing journey. This spiritual connection has offered me a sense of continuity and belonging.

F.   Shadow work with ancestors: Delving into the shadow aspects of our lineage to foster deep healing. I am a huge advocate of Shadow work within wytchcraft. Shadow work with ancestors involves exploring the less visible or acknowledged aspects of our ancestry, including unresolved traumas, conflicts, and negative patterns. By addressing these hidden elements, I have found that I have been able to achieve deeper healing and transformation. This process has allowed me to recognize and release inherited burdens and hurts, leading me to personal growth and a healthier relationship with myself and my kin. It has been a profound way for me to heal, not only from my own wounds but also from patterns that may have been passed down through generations.

Exercise: "Exploring Ancestral Patterns"

Objective: This exercise helps you recognize and understand potential ancestral patterns or "curses" that may have been passed down through generations, empowering you to break free from negative cycles.

Instructions:
   1. Self-Reflection:
   Find a quiet and comfortable space where you can reflect on your life and family history without distractions.
   2. Ancestral Patterns:
   Begin by considering any recurring negative patterns or challenges that you've noticed within your family or even in your own life. These pat-

terns might include financial struggles, relationship issues, health concerns, or emotional challenges.

3. Journaling:

Open a journal or create a digital document dedicated to this exercise.

Write down any patterns you've identified, both within your family and in your personal experiences. Be specific and detailed in your descriptions.

4. Family Stories:

Reach out to family members, such as parents, grandparents, or aunts and uncles, to gather insights into the family's history. Ask about challenges or difficulties they or previous generations have faced.

5. Additional Patterns:

Record any additional ancestral patterns or stories shared by your family members. Include historical context if available.

6. Analysis:

Review the patterns you've documented. Consider how they might be interconnected or influenced by historical events, cultural factors, or family dynamics.

7. Self-Reflection:

Reflect on whether you've experienced any of these patterns in your own life. Be honest with yourself about their impact on your well-being and happiness.

8. Breaking the Cycle:

Now, brainstorm ways to break free from these patterns. What steps can you take to avoid repeating negative behaviors or outcomes in your life?

Consider seeking professional support, therapy, or counseling if necessary to help you work through these patterns.

9. Positive Affirmations:

Create a list of positive affirmations or intentions that counteract the negative patterns you've identified. These can serve as reminders to choose a different path.

10. Empowerment:

Embrace the idea that you have the power to change the course of your life and your family's history. You are not bound by ancestral patterns, and you can create a brighter future.

11. Continued Awareness:

Commit to ongoing self-awareness and vigilance in recognizing and addressing any negative patterns that may emerge in your life.

Let's Do the Working:

Ancestral Ritual for Healing Personal Trauma

Materials Needed:
  – A small table or altar
  – A white candle
  – A piece of paper and pen
  – Fresh flowers or herbs
  – A small bowl of water
  – A photo or representation of an ancestor (if available)

Steps:

1. Setting the Space: Choose a quiet and comfortable space where you can focus without interruption. Place the small table or altar in front of you.

2. Creating Sacred Space: Light the white candle at the center of the table. This candle represents purity, healing, and the connection between the physical and spiritual realms.

3. Invoking Ancestral Presence: If you have a photo or representation of an ancestor, place it on the table. If not, simply speak aloud, addressing

your ancestors. Say, "To my ancestors, those who came before me, I invite your loving presence and guidance."

4. Centering Yourself: Close your eyes, take a few deep breaths, and imagine a warm and supportive light surrounding you. Feel a sense of comfort and safety as you connect with the energy of your ancestors.

5. Writing Your Intentions: Take the piece of paper and pen. Write down the personal trauma or pain you wish to heal. Acknowledge the feelings associated with it. Be honest and vulnerable in your words.

6. Connecting with Ancestral Wisdom: Hold the paper in your hands and imagine the support of your ancestors enveloping you. Visualize their wisdom, resilience, and love. Ask them to guide you through your healing journey.

7. Releasing: Hold the paper over the candle's flame (but not too close) and say, "With the power of fire, I release the hold this trauma has had on me. Let it transform into ashes, clearing space for healing."

8. Cleansing: Dip your fingers into the bowl of water and sprinkle a few drops onto the paper. As you do, imagine the water purifying and cleansing the pain you've written. Say, "With the essence of water, I cleanse and purify this pain, allowing healing waters to flow through me."

9. Connecting with Nature: Place the fresh flowers or herbs on the altar. These represent the cycles of life, growth, and renewal. Visualize yourself growing and healing, just as nature does.

10. Affirmation: Repeat a healing affirmation to yourself, such as "I am worthy of healing and peace" or "I release the pain and embrace my own strength."

11. Offering Gratitude: Express your gratitude to your ancestors for their support. Say, "Thank you, dear ancestors, for your love and guidance as I heal."

12. Closing: Gently blow out the candle, knowing that the energy of your ancestors and the ritual's intention will continue to support your healing journey.

13. Continuing Healing: Keep the paper with you or burn it in a safe place. You can revisit this ritual whenever you need to reinforce your healing intentions.

This ritual is a way to connect with the wisdom and strength of your ancestors as you navigate your healing process. It can be deeply meaningful and cathartic, but if you find that your trauma is overwhelming or persistent, seeking the help of a mental health professional is essential.

CHAPTER SIX
WALKING THE MAGICKAL
PATH WITHOUT FEAR

"Allow Yourself to be afraid, for fear is a natural companion on the path of progress. But don't let fear paralyze you. Instead, let it ignite the fire within, propelling you to move forward with unwavering courage and determination."

Magick and witchcraft are paths that have fascinated humanity for centuries. It is seen as a journey of self-discovery, transformation, and connection with forces beyond the material world. Yet, for many, the word 'magick' evokes images of secrecy, danger, and fear. In this chapter, I will explore the idea of walking the magickal path without fear by diving into its essence and offering guidance on how I personally have navigated my own fears to be able to walk this path with confidence and respect.

The fear of the unknown has always been a human trait. It is the fear of what we don't understand, the fear of losing control, and the fear of consequences. Magick, with its mysteries and its ability to reshape reality, naturally invokes fear in those who are unfamiliar with it. However, fear should never be the driving force behind your magickal practice. Instead, it should be a source of curiosity, respect, and inspiration.

Growing up with my mom was a baptism by fire when it came to fear. She lived in a constant state of worry and fear. She moved away from that way of thinking as she got older (she would tell me later that it was because she watched me walk headfirst into things that scared me to death). I do remember, though, that when I was little, she was afraid of everything. She was afraid of thunder. She was afraid of bugs. She was afraid that we would wander too far from the house. She was just afraid.

The thing that I have noticed about people who live their lives in fear, is that many times that fear is past down to those who spend time with them. The one phrase I remember my mom using most was, "Don't make eye contact." Now there were particular people or groups of people this was directed toward…strangers, in particular, but also those who others categorized as mentally challenge, homeless people, and stray animals.

Ma never felt comfortable around any of those things. It makes me wonder what might have happened in her youth to trigger that much fear. As you can imagine, many of Ma's fears began to take root in me as I grew up being exposed to them. I remember a group of mentally challenged teens who attended my elementary school…I would see them coming, and I could feel my whole body go rigid. I would silently pray that they would stay far from me. Had they given me any reason to fear them? No. It was all something that I had concocted in my own head that caused that fear.

I also remember, as a young'un, walking toward a stray dog that came into our yard. I can still hear Ma yelling out from the front door, "Don't you touch that dog! It might have the mange!" Now, at that time, I had absolutely no clue what 'the mange' was, but I was sure I didn't want it. So I ran. It was then that a fear of stray dogs tried to creep in.

In my hometown, there was a local homeless woman, Crazy Mary. Ma had heard stories of how Mary went crazy because she had always wanted children. When she miscarried after her first and only pregnancy, it drove her to the depths of insanity, and she walked the streets looking for a child to call her own. I never knew if any of the stories were true, but I know that because of Ma's fearful nature, we steered clear of her.

I carried many of these fears with me through grade school, high school, and even part of college. When I passed a homeless person, Ma's voice would ring clear in the back of my mind, "Don't make eye contact!" When I worked at a local grocery store back home, the adults from the local group home would come in once a week to do their shopping. I always made a bee-line for the stock room with my mom's mantra ringing in my ears, "Don't make eye contact!"

I have found, in my own life, that one of the most potent tools for dispelling fear is knowledge. Understanding the principles and history behind anything normally helps to take the fire out of that fear. I have found it to be much the same with magickal practices. I have found, through study and exposure, that magick becomes far less intimidating and scary.

I have also found that fear often rises up from within ourselves. It is often rooted in our own doubts and insecurities. One of the things that one of my dear friends taught me was to always go into magick introspectively. In these processes, I have explored my own fears and doubts, acknowledging them and working through them.

Ma has always told me that I was the hard headed one in the family. I have never been the type of person who wanted to be limited by anything, most of all, myself, so I made it a point to put myself into situations where I had to address those fears. Again, this wasn't done with wild abandon and a frivolous nature. It was done with much soul-searching and thought.

The first fear I worked to overcome was that fear of those that others called mentally challenged. When I was in school in Knoxville, Tennessee, I had to work to be able to afford school, so I worked full-time evenings in a local bookstore, but on weekends, I worked at a facility for adults with learning, mental, and physical challenges.

My first five minutes in that facility were pure hell for me. I broke out in cold sweats and shook continuously. My biggest fear, looking back now, is that someone might have actually talked to me. My first duty was to help to clean a young fellow up after he finished his meal. He laughed and smiled at me the whole time. It made me feel ashamed of the fears I had held onto for so many years. I looked in his eyes and saw joy...pure elation that someone was spending time with him and helping him. He looked at me and smiled even bigger. I could feel a tear work its way down my cheek, and then I felt his hand against my face. "No cry...happy...happy." He laughed out loud as heartily as he could, and that laugh touched me so much that I couldn't help but join him.

I turned around, and there was a woman in her forties standing almost close enough to me that I could feel her breath on my face. "I love you!" The worker beside me leaned in and whispered, "That's her thing. She loves everybody. She will tell you at least 100 times a day." I smiled at her. Again, she says, "I love you!" I was a bit perplexed. I leaned toward her and said, "I love you too." She looked at me in shock, and quietly whispered, "For real?!" So I whispered back, "For real." She smiled from ear to ear. Each day after, we had that same exchange with her only saying "I love you" once and then waiting for the response.

I have also found, in my life and my magickal practice, that fear has a way of confronting you just to see how you are going to react. This country boy from rural North Carolina who was scared to death of getting 'the mange' moved to Atlanta, and the only job I could find was a job at a veterinary clinic. Of course, one of the first cases I had to assist with was.... yep, you guessed it...THE MANGE. I was frozen in my tracks when the vet asked me to hold the dog for the examination. I had latex gloves everywhere I could put them. I had suited up like I was going into a plague. It was at this point that the doctor decided that I needed to know the difference between demodectic mange and sarcoptic mange. After this, I knew what precautions to take and how to treat 'the mange' so the fears were gone.

My mother's fears have tried so hard to take root in me...I was in New York City in 1985. I was being shown around the city by a friend who had moved there six months prior. I was told adamantly that you don't touch or engage the pigeons and the homeless. "They are like rats (the pigeons and the homeless folks). You can't be nice to them...they will follow you everywhere."

Years later, when I was working with the Assemblies of God church, I was asked to be a part of a homeless ministry that cooked breakfast and served it on the streets underneath a bridge. I got to know and became friends with many of those people who gathered under that bridge to eat. As I talked to one fellow, I found out that he was my age and he had missed one paycheck. Not so different from me at all.

While fear should never be the driving force behind anything, it should definitely never be that force behind a magickal practice. Yes, it is essential to take precautions and practice grounding and protection techniques. These ensure that you are in a safe and empowered state when you engage in your magickal workings. Intuition plays a strong part of this equation. Pay attention to your intuition and to the energies around you. Magick often will communicate through subtle signs and messages. Trust your own instincts and be open to the unexpected.

I often find it funny. Over the years, the most powerful magick I have ever found were in the things of which my own mother was most afraid. I found magick in the eyes of those whose minds danced differently than my own. I found magick in the eyes of animals whose hearts were far purer than my own. I found magick in the eyes of those who used the earth as their pillow and the stars as their nightlight and I can say without hesitation, I am far richer for all of it.

Ultimately, magick is a path of personal growth and transformation and it challenges us to confront our own limitations, to expand our consciousness, and to cultivate a deeper connection with the universe. I love the quote by author Ambrose Hollingworth Redmoon, "Courage is not the absence of fear, but rather the judgment that something else is more important than fear."

As witches and magickal practitioners, we can't let fear rule us. We are the ones who walk the liminal spaces. We were born out of extraordinary and all things unexplained. Walking the magickal path without fear is a journey of self-reflection, responsibility, and growth. Fear may linger in the shadows, but it should never be the guiding force in our magickal journey. If we embrace the magick and move past the fear, it will empower us to become the best, most magickal version of ourselves.

Exercise: "Exploring Your Fears"

Objective: This exercise is designed to help you recognize and better understand your fears, providing a foundation for personal growth and self-awareness.

Instructions:
1. Quiet Space:

Find a quiet and comfortable space where you can reflect and write without interruptions.

2. Journal or Notebook:

Have a journal, notebook, or digital document ready to record your thoughts and observations.

3. Deep Breathing:

Begin with a few deep breaths to relax your mind and body. Inhale deeply through your nose and exhale slowly through your mouth.

4. Fear Identification:

Start by making a list of any fears or anxieties that come to mind. These can be specific fears or general worries. Write them down without judgment.

5. Childhood Reflection:

Reflect on your childhood and upbringing. Were there any significant events or experiences that may have contributed to the development of these fears? Write about these experiences in detail.

6. Triggers:

Think about what triggers your fears in the present. Are there specific situations, people, or thoughts that intensify your fears? Write down any triggers you can identify.

7. Emotional Responses:

For each fear you've listed, describe the emotional responses or physical sensations you experience when confronted with that fear. Consider how it affects your thoughts and behaviors.

8. Rational Analysis:

Analyze each fear from a rational perspective. Are these fears based on reality or rooted in irrational thoughts or beliefs? Challenge the validity of each fear.

9. Coping Strategies:

Write down any coping strategies or techniques you've used to deal with these fears in the past. Evaluate their effectiveness and whether they help or hinder your progress.

10. Support System:

Consider who in your life can provide support or guidance in addressing these fears. Whether it's friends, family, a therapist, or support groups, identify your sources of support.

11. Positive Affirmations:

Create a list of positive affirmations or statements that counteract your fears. These affirmations can serve as reminders of your strength and resilience.

12. Commit to Action:

Choose one fear from your list that you're ready to confront or work on. Set a specific and achievable goal related to that fear. This could be a small step towards facing it.

13. Regular Reflection:

Commit to regular reflection and journaling about your progress. Document any changes in your thoughts, emotions, or behaviors as you address your fears.

14. Self-Compassion:

Throughout this process, practice self-compassion and kindness toward yourself. Recognize that facing fears is a courageous journey, and setbacks are a natural part of growth.

Let's Do the Working:

Ritual: From Fear to Freedom

Items Needed:
1. A small, smooth stone
2. A body of water (river, creek, lake, ocean) or a fire-safe container filled with water
3. A quiet, outdoor space

The Working:
1. Choose Your Location:

Find a peaceful and natural outdoor setting where you can perform this ritual. Ensure you won't be disturbed.

2. Center Yourself:

Stand or sit comfortably and take a few deep breaths to center your energy. Feel the connection between yourself and the earth.

3. Hold the Stone:

Hold the smooth stone in your hand. This stone will represent the fears you wish to release.

4. Reflect on Your Fears:

Close your eyes and bring to mind the fear or fears that you want to release. Allow yourself to feel these emotions without judgment.

5. Transfer Fears to the Stone:

Imagine the fears flowing from your body and into the stone in your hand. Visualize it as energy leaving you and entering the stone.

6. Offer Your Fear to the Elements:

If you're near a body of water, gently toss the stone into the water, symbolizing the release of your fear into the flowing currents.

If you're not near water, you can instead bury the stone in the earth, returning it to the ground.

7. Watch and Reflect:

As the stone sinks in the water or is buried in the earth, observe it as it becomes one with the natural elements. Reflect on the freedom you feel as these fears leave your life.

8. Affirmation and Freedom:

Speak an affirmation aloud. This is one that I wrote:

In the silence of this sacred space,
I release my fear, let it find its place.
With courage rising, I take this chance,
To banish fear's grip, with intention's dance.
I cast away doubt, I cast away fright,
Embracing the day and the tranquil night.
With every word of this spell I say,
I release my fears, I send them away.
No longer imprisoned by what holds me back,
I walk a new path, on a fearless track.
In the light of hope, I now appear,
For I've chanted this spell to release my fear.

9. Feel the Freedom:

Close your eyes and take a moment to fully embrace the sense of freedom that comes with releasing your fear. Feel the lightness and peace in your heart.

10. Connect with Nature:

Spend some quiet moments connecting with the natural surroundings. Listen to the sounds of the wind, water, or the earth beneath you. Feel the support and wisdom of nature.

11. Closing:

Express gratitude for the opportunity to release fear and embrace freedom. Know that this process is ongoing and that you are now on a path of liberation.

12. Return:

When you're ready, return to your everyday awareness, knowing that you've taken a significant step towards letting go of fear and welcoming freedom into your life.

Repeat this ritual whenever you feel the need to release fear or negativity and reconnect with the freedom that resides within you and the natural world. It's a simple yet powerful way to find peace and liberation.

CHAPTER SEVEN
THE MAGICK OF
ENCOURAGEMENT

"Never try to diminish the magick of another, for each soul's
potential is unique and powerful. Fan the flames of passion. Feed
the fire of inspiration. Together, we will illuminate the world."

In the realm of magick, there exists a powerful force often overlooked, one
that can shape destinies, mend broken spirits, and bring forth greatness in
the most unexpected of places. This force is a simple concept called encouragement. Encouragement is not merely a fleeting sentiment; it is a potent
spell that can transform lives and kindle the fires of inspiration in others.

At its core, encouragement is the art of using our words and gestures to
uplift and motivate others. Just as a skilled alchemist transforms base met-
als into gold, the adept encourager changes doubt and despair into hope
and determination. Words are the tools of this transformation, and when
combined with intention, they can work wonders.

The magick of encouragement relies on the choice of words. Positive
language can be likened to a well-crafted spell. It has the power to push
away darkness and summon light. Phrases like "I believe in you," "You are
capable," and "You've got this" can be the spells that unlock hidden potential and set forth a cascade of positive change.

Encouragement often takes the form of affirmations, which can be
used as spells that we weave for ourselves and others. Repeating affirma-

tions can build confidence and reshape reality. For instance, "I am strong" or "I am worthy" are words that, when repeated with conviction, can summon strength and worthiness.

One of the remarkable aspects of the magick of encouragement is its ability to create a ripple effect. When you encourage someone, you not only impact their life but also set in motion a chain reaction of positivity. This ripple effect extends far beyond what the eye can see. I often compare this to skipping rocks on a creek or lake. As you carefully plan the speed, force, and direction you are throwing the rock, it creates movement and affects anything that is touches or comes in contact with. That is the way I see the magick of encouragement. As we form our words and actions, the way we use them can affect change…it can create movement within the person being encouraged. If you think about it, most of the time all we need to stir our own passion is for someone else to believe in and to support us. Encouragement boosts confidence, which in turn empowers individuals to take bold actions they might have otherwise shied away from. A simple word of encouragement can be the catalyst for someone to pursue their dreams or overcome their fears.

In the face of adversity, I like to envision that encouragement acts much like a shield. It provides the strength needed to weather the storms that we face and keeps us moving forward. Just as a spell of protection wards off harm, encouragement can help to protect the spirit from doubt and despair. Every day, we are constantly beaten down by words (either the words of others or even our own). Some of the harshest criticism we hear comes from our own mouths. I know for a fact that I can be my own harshest critic. I have tried as I have gotten older to be conscious of what I say about myself and others…even in a joking manner.

To harness and become adept at the magick of encouragement, one must embody the role of the encourager with sincerity and empathy. The encourager offers support and guidance, all while respecting the freedom and boundaries of the individual. Encouragement often begins with active listening. By tuning in to the concerns and dreams of others, the encourager gains insight into how best to provide support. Listening is akin to divination, where hidden truths can be unveiled. Along that same vein of thought, the encourager is not just a cheerleader but a guide who offers constructive feedback. Just as a mentor imparts wisdom and guidance, the encourager provides valuable insights that help others grow and evolve. The encourager, again, needs to respect the boundaries of the one they are encouraging and only offer guidance or advice if asked.

As with any magick, the power of encouragement should be used ethically and responsibly. While encouragement can work wonders, it should never be used to manipulate or deceive. True encouragement is based on authenticity and genuine care for the well-being of others. It's important to respect the boundaries and choices of those you seek to encourage. Everyone's journey is unique, and not all paths are the same. Encouragement should be offered as a gift, not an imposition. This is a sticky situation… some people truly don't want someone offering them encouragement. The way this can be approached, if you aren't certain, is to offer encouragement, and if that person isn't receptive, honor their position and move on.

Just as too much of a certain medication can have adverse effects, excessive encouragement can lead to dependency or a false sense of security. Encourage, but also allow room for self-discovery and growth. In offering encouragement, it is important not to create an atmosphere of codependency. Our goal as an encourager is just that, to encourage. The meaning of encouragement is to give support or to stimulate motivation so that the person being encouraged can walk it out on their own. We can't make decisions or walk the path for them. We can be there to walk alongside of them and help them to see their own talents and abilities and help them to find ways to nurture those parts of themselves.

The magick of encouragement is a powerful force that has the potential to transform lives and create a more compassionate and supportive world. As practitioners of this magick, we hold the key to unlocking the hidden potentials within ourselves and others, bringing forth the light of inspiration and the promise of a brighter future. Through our words and actions, we can continue to weave the enchantment of encouragement, empowering individuals to reach for the stars and achieve their wildest dreams. Help others to see their own power, their own adeptness. Give them a glimpse of the potential and beauty that you see in them, but let them walk in it.

Encouragement isn't about giving blind praise. It isn't about building up someone's ego. Encouragement is about adding fuel to an existing action, state of mind, or belief. When I encourage, I try to inspire with courage, spirit, and hope. When I offer encouragement, it is to remind someone of just how valuable they are and how much they personally have to offer... the world, the community, even themselves. I don't offer empty compliments or words. That practice in itself can be seen through. The words come across as plastic and artificial. When you truly encourage someone, they can feel the energy flow through you and into them, offering them the motivation to put themselves out there with confidence.

In my practice, I choose not to see other wytches or magick folk as competition. There is too much of that in the world as it is. I am one who wants to see everyone win. Your success is my success and vice versa. Life is already far too hard to feel like I am constantly trying to stay ahead of or to worry about rivalries and feuds. As I get older, I realize that these things don't matter and don't deserve my energy. I would rather spend my time offering encouragement to others and see them walking as the most magickal being that they can be. My dear friend Cindy Maluna said it best, "Just concentrate on being the wytch that you are. Send out magick, and magick is what you'll get back." I feel the same about the Magick of Encouragement. If I send encouragement out, then I will certainly get it back...not necessarily flattery or being the recipient of endless adulation. I believe in heartfelt sentiment. Honestly, offering words to build someone up and helping them to see the power and the beauty within themselves.

Exercise: "Spotting Opportunities for Encouragement"

Objective: This exercise encourages you to actively seek and create opportunities to uplift and encourage those around you, fostering positive connections and making a difference in their lives.

Instructions:

1. Mindful Awareness:

Find a quiet and contemplative space to reflect on your interactions with others.

2. Journal or Notebook:

Have a journal or notebook ready to record your observations and experiences.

3. Setting Intentions:

Begin by setting your intention for this exercise: to actively seek opportunities to encourage and support others.

4. Reflect on Your Circles:

Think about the various circles in your life—family, friends, co-workers, acquaintances, or even strangers you encounter regularly. Reflect on the people you interact with regularly or occasionally.

5. Identifying Needs:

For each circle or group of people, consider the potential needs, challenges, or goals they might have. What are some common stressors or aspirations within these groups?

6. Active Listening:

Practice active listening when you engage with people. Pay close attention to their words, emotions, and body language. Try to understand their feelings and perspectives.

7. Genuine Compliments:

Look for opportunities to offer sincere compliments. Acknowledge someone's strengths, accomplishments, or positive qualities. A genuine compliment can brighten someone's day.

8. Supportive Words:

Offer words of support, encouragement, or empathy when someone shares their challenges or concerns. Let them know you're there for them and believe in their abilities.

9. Acts of Kindness:

Perform small acts of kindness, such as helping a coworker with a task, offering to run an errand for a neighbor, or surprising a friend with a thoughtful gesture. These actions can be powerful sources of encouragement.

10. Positive Feedback:

When appropriate, provide constructive and positive feedback. Let someone know when they've done a great job or made progress towards their goals.

11. Celebrate Achievements:

Celebrate the achievements and milestones of those around you. Whether it's a promotion, a personal achievement, or a special occasion, join in their joy and show your support.

12. Empathetic Listening:

Practice empathetic listening when someone is going through a difficult time. Sometimes, offering a compassionate ear can be the most encouraging act.

13. Self-Reflection:

Periodically reflect on your experiences. How did your words and actions impact others? How did it make you feel to encourage and support those around you?

14. Repeat and Expand:

Continue to actively seek and create opportunities for encouragement in your daily interactions. Expand your circle of influence by seeking opportunities to encourage strangers or members of your community.

15. Gratitude:

Cultivate gratitude for the positive connections and meaningful relationships you build through encouragement. Recognize the joy and fulfillment that comes from uplifting others.

Let's Do the Working:

Ritual for the Magick of Encouragement: "The Luminary Blessing"

This ritual is designed for you to channel the magick of encouragement and send positive, empowering energy to others. Whether you wish to uplift a friend, family member, or anyone in need of support, this ritual will help you manifest your intentions for their well-being. I always ask the person I am including in the working if it is ok for me to do the working for them. I don't want to infringe on their will.

Materials Needed:
   – A quiet, sacred space
   – A white candle
   – A photograph or representation of the person you want to encourage
   – A piece of paper and a pen
   – Crystals (optional, for added energy. Quartz is always a good all purpose crystal)
   – Essential oils (use uplifting scents. I like to use citrus scents and mint)
   – A comfortable chair or cushion

Preparation:
   1. Choose a time and location where you won't be disturbed during the ritual. Dim the lights and create a peaceful atmosphere.
   2. Set up your sacred space by placing the white candle, photograph or representation, paper, and pen on a table or altar. You can also arrange

crystals around the table for added energy.

3. If you have essential oils, anoint the candle with a few drops while focusing on your intention for the ritual. Imagine the oil infusing the candle with positive energy.

The Ritual:

1. Begin by taking a few moments to center yourself. Close your eyes, take deep breaths, and visualize a radiant white light surrounding you.

2. Light the white candle, symbolizing purity and positivity. As you do, say:

"With this candle's light, I invoke the power of encouragement and support for [person's name]. May their path be illuminated with confidence and resilience."

3. Place the photograph or representation of the person in front of you. Gaze upon it with a loving and compassionate heart, connecting with their energy and essence.

4. Take the piece of paper and write down heartfelt words of encouragement and positivity for the person. Share your belief in their abilities and potential. Be specific and sincere in your message.

5. Hold the paper to your heart and visualize your words of encouragement as a radiant, golden energy. Feel this energy filling the paper and imbuing it with your intention.

6. Hold the paper over the candle's flame, allowing it to catch fire. As it burns, say:

"As this paper turns to ash, so do any doubts or fears that [person's name] may carry. May they rise with a luminous spirit, filled with strength and determination."

Safely extinguish the burning paper in a fireproof dish or container.

7. Continue to focus on the person's representation, imagining them bathed in a warm, glowing light, symbolizing your support and encourage-

ment. Visualize them becoming more confident and motivated.

8. If you have crystals, hold them in your hand or place them near the photograph while visualizing your positive energy flowing toward the person.

Closing:

After completing the ritual, sit in silence for a few moments, feeling the energy of encouragement and support surrounding you. You can repeat this ritual as needed, always respecting the well-being of the person you are encouraging. Your heartfelt blessings and intentions can have a profound and uplifting impact on their life.

CHAPTER EIGHT
UNLEASH THE WILD
WITHIN

"Embrace that untamed part of yourself, the wild man who
isn't afraid to take risks, who revels in the thrill of life. Let go of
inhibitions and let him run free, for within his passionate spirit
lies the courage to live authentically. It's about finding the balance
between responsibility and unbridled freedom, honoring the primal
energy that reminds us of the raw beauty in simply being alive."

In the hustle and bustle of our everyday lives, it's easy to forget that deep
within us, there exists a wild and untamed part of our souls. Call it the wild
man, the primal self, or simply an inner spark of adventure – it's that part
of our being that often gets buried beneath layers of responsibility and rou-
tine. But what if we were to rediscover and embrace this untamed spirit?
What if we allowed it to run free, like a herd of wild horses?

Let's be honest; life can be boring at times. We follow routines, meet
deadlines, and navigate the expectations of society. Our inhibitions become
like a tight collar, restraining us from embracing our truest selves. Yet, if we
peel away these layers, we uncover a part of us that's alive, fearless, and willing to take risks. It's the wild man, that fearless adventurer who relishes the
thrill of living.

There's something exhilarating about taking risks. It's like stepping to
the edge of a cliff, heart pounding, and leaping into the unknown. The

wild man within us understands that life is an adventure and that some-times, the best stories come from those daring moments. Whether it's pur-suing an uncharted career path, traveling to a distant land, or opening up to someone new, risks are the threads that weave the fabric of our most exciting tales.

Living authentically means allowing the wild man to have his say. It's about finding that balance between responsibility and unbridled freedom. We don't need to abandon our commitments but rather infuse them with the vitality of our untamed spirit. When we do this, life takes on new di-mensions. It becomes an art, a dance, an expression of our true selves.

In the heart of our wild nature, we find a primal energy that connects us to the very essence of existence. It reminds us that we are part of the grand scheme of life, purposefully placed in the natural world. Just as a wolf runs through the wilderness with instinctual grace, we too can navigate the complexities of life when we honor this primal energy.

Ultimately, embracing the untamed part of ourselves is a celebration of the raw beauty in simply being alive. It's about waking up each day with a sense of wonder, knowing that life is a gift. It's about looking at the world through the eyes of the wild man and seeing the extraordinary in the or-dinary.

So, as you read this, remember that within you resides a wild man or woman, ready to remind you of the exhilaration of existence. Embrace that untamed spirit, let it breathe life into your days, and savor the journey of living authentically, with courage, and in awe of the world's untamed beauty.

How do I keep that wild and feral nature alive in my own practice? I spend time with the wild and the feral. I spend as much time as I possibly can in the woods. I find that if I am not able to engage that wild part of my spirit that I feel listless, emotionless and stagnant. It may be as simple as going into the woods on my lunch and taking a nap under one of the old oaks. It could be a hike at Red Top Mountain…or it could just be running through the woods, releasing my inhibitions, and dancing as hard as I can under the canopy of trees.

I have found, in times like these, that the wind makes a wonderful dance partner. As a part of the corporate world, I have found that too much time spent behind the screen of a computer makes me feel compromised…far too domesticated…tame. Disappearing into a canvas of green helps me to push those feelings…and yes, that attitude, out of my Craft. In these excursions into nature, I find myself feeling that wild, uninhibited, and even feral part of my spirit rising to meet the spirits of nature as they move around and in me.

It seems that as I navigate social media, that I find so much promotion of a 'user-friendly and safe' version of the Craft. Even personally, I have found myself doing things that made wytchcraft more palatable to my friends and acquaintances outside of the magickal path. For a while, my trips to the woods became less than productive and I found myself offering a 'gingerbread house' type of magick (appealing and appetizing to those looking in from the outside). We all have those fluffy love and light moments, and there is a need for the sweet, calm magickal moments, but there is also that part my path that thrives when I work with bones and baneful plants. I crave the old ways, and I find freedom in dancing naked among the trees, plants, and creatures around me.

Over the years, I have made it my purpose to incorporate more of that part of myself into my magick. I have found that bearing my teeth and adding bite back into my practices have made my magick more real…more authentic. As I grew in my magickal journey, I found that in trying to sand off my rough, jagged edges that I was also rendering my intention toothless.

As of late, my trips to the woods have begun to take flight under cover of nightfall…when the moon is bright and beckoning me to join in its dance. Bathed in darkness and in the silence of midnight, not only am I able to shed my clothing, but my inhibitions as well. My backpack, typically loaded down with tools for the workings planned—my spirit primed and ready to release the energy and passion into each element of my workings—I feel at home.

I have found, in this time, that I am visited more by the creatures of the woods who tend to hide or sleep during the day. I have encountered my old friends… foxes, raccoons, owls, and, of course, my old comrade, the opossum. I realize that there are lessons to be learned from this animal, and I have put much effort into overcoming the fear that this giant grimacing creature instills in me. I know that they are essentially harmless to humans and are beneficial, and they aren't carriers of rabies…but still, that toothy rat-like, ambling beast makes me cringe. Such a wonderful visual of the feral, wild, wytch, huh? With each encounter, I try to learn by observing these fascinating creatures. The fox is constantly watching, ears pricked for any sound around him and thinking only of the next steps he must take. The owl, eyes and head constantly moving, searching the ground for other animals that will quench his hunger and give him the strength needed.

I have grown tired of being 'safe' and 'palatable' in my magick. I am okay with people being watchful and even a bit leery when they are around me. I want the full nature of my Craft and practices to emanate from my being/ spirit/soul. It is imperative that my magick include light, dark, and the gray. I grow tired some days of being positively civilized and I hunger for that which feeds my wild heart.

I think for this reason, alone, I crave the thorny, sweaty, uninhibited dance with the nature spirits. I want to be able to extend my teeth and claws in the company of other who understand the hunger for the unfettered. Through observation of the creatures around me during my midnight romps in the woods, I have come to realize that the teeth and claws only show when necessary.

Daily life is stressful enough; our magickal journey should not be. It should be a culmination of all that we are…the good, the bad, and yes, even the ugly. My strongest magick comes out of passion, fear, frustration, and even anger. I have been learning over the course of the last couple of years to embrace my fears. My fear can prove at any point in time to be my strongest ally.

In all of my soul searching, I have come to realize that the thing that I am most afraid of is myself. I have been afraid to let myself run free...in complete abandon. I have lived so much of my life afraid of what others might think of me. My fears have always been an unknown yet familiar force that not only can hold me prisoner but will also hunt me down if I give it any headway.

I know now that fear isn't the ruling force in my life. It is a companion that spurs me on to walk and even run outside of the parameters of my own comfort zone. I worked as a pastor in the mainline Christian churches for over ten years, and fear was seen as a 'check' for the spirit. If you felt fear, it was your soul telling you not to do or say or try something. As I have approached my sage years, I have realized that this isn't what fear is at all. I know now that fear is essentially an unpleasant and often strong emotion caused by the *anticipation* of danger. That one word is the key there. Anticipation. Fear is a mechanism built into us to protect ourselves.

I use fear now as a motivator. When I feel it trying to rear its head, I check myself first to see if the fear is truly warranted. If I determine that the feeling is just my own emotions flailing to keep me comfortable, I will typically move forward with whatever opportunity or task is presented. I realized that in my youth and in my young adulthood that I had built many walls to protect myself. Once I began to tear down those walls, I realized that it was fear that was crippling me.

Now I feel like I need to put a disclaimer in here. I can feel MawMaw staring over my shoulder. This isn't a license for stupidity. I am not telling you that if you are afraid of heights to go jump out of a barn loft. I am not telling you that if you are afraid of bears to go into the woods looking for one. I am telling you that you need to get some gumption about yourself and move beyond yourself and experience life and the world around you.

I am, by nature, an introvert. I am not comfortable in crowds. I don't do well starting conversations. My job, my life, and my magickal path in general have forced me to be an extroverted introvert. In this case, fear was my motivator. I realized that to do what was required of me in work, magick, and in life in general, I had to get over myself...literally. I had to take all of that fear of interaction and all of the inhibitions and overcome it. This is where the wild man in me had to take over. At first, it was just about walking it out. I forced myself to do things that were uncomfortable. I made myself walk outside of the scope of fear. At some point, this new boldness became a part of me. I learned that fear was no longer the ruling factor in my life. It was just a checkpoint. It was in this realization that boldness and strength took root. It is in this realization that I found my teeth and claws.

When we feel overcome by fear and overwhelmed by the daily grind, it is important to remember that, like a wild spirit, untamed and free, you are a force of nature, unbridled by conventions and limitations. Your energy flows like a rushing river, unpredictable and adventurous, carving its unique path through the landscape of life. Just as the wind whispers secrets to the trees and the stars illuminate the night sky, your untamed spirit adds magick to this world, reminding us all of the beauty in spontaneity and the untamed nature of existence.

Exercise: "Exploring Your Inner Wild Person"

Objective: This exercise invites you to reconnect with your primal and untamed nature, embracing the wild aspects of yourself that may have been suppressed or forgotten.

Instructions:

    1. Nature Connection:

        Find a natural setting that resonates with you, whether it's a forest, a park, a beach, or even your own backyard. This will be your sanctuary for this exercise.

2. Digital Detox:

Leave behind electronic devices, if possible. This exercise is about immersing yourself in nature without distractions.

3. Wilderness Journal:

Bring a journal or notebook and a pen to document your experience.

4. Mindful Arrival:

As you enter your chosen natural space, take a moment to pause and breathe deeply. Consciously leave behind the stresses and responsibilities of everyday life.

5. The Five Senses:

Engage your senses fully. Close your eyes and listen to the sounds around you—the rustling leaves, birdsong, or the rush of water. Touch the earth beneath your feet and notice its texture. Breathe in deeply and savor the scents of the natural world. Open your eyes and observe the colors, shapes, and details of your surroundings. Taste a small piece of edible plant if you're in a safe environment.

6. Wild Movement:

Allow yourself to move freely and intuitively. Walk, run, dance, or simply let your body sway to the rhythm of nature. Feel the exhilaration of unstructured movement.

7. Animal Imitation:

Embrace your inner wildness by imitating the movements and sounds of animals you encounter or feel drawn to. Become the deer grazing, the bird in flight, or the river flowing. Let go of self-consciousness and embody the creatures of the wild.

8. Earth Connection:

Find a comfortable spot to sit or lie down on the ground. Feel the earth beneath you, and visualize your energy merging with the earth's energy. Imagine roots extending from your body into the ground, anchoring you to the earth.

9. Inner Dialogue:

- In your journal, write about the sensations, emotions, and insights that arise during your time in nature. Reflect on how you felt when you allowed your inner wild person to surface.

10. Primal Roar:

If you feel comfortable and are in a secluded space, let out a primal roar or yell. Release any pent-up energy and emotions, allowing yourself to be fully present and untamed.

11. Natural Art:

Engage in creative expression using materials you find in nature. Build a small sculpture, create a mandala with leaves and stones, or paint with natural pigments if available.

12. Express Gratitude:

As you prepare to leave your natural sanctuary, express gratitude to the wildness within and around you. Offer a silent thank-you to the earth and the elements for this transformative experience.

13. Integration:

Carry the sense of your inner wild person with you as you return to your daily life. Embrace the courage, freedom, and untamed energy that you've reconnected with during this exercise.

Let's Do the Working:

Ritual for Rewylding the Spirit

Materials Needed:

– A quiet natural setting (forest, park, garden, or any place with natural surroundings).

– A journal and pen.

– A small token or offering for nature (such as a flower or stone).

– Comfortable clothing suitable for the outdoors, or you can be un-clothed.

– Optional: Candle and lighter for indoor adaptation.

Preparation:

Choose a time for your ritual when you can be alone and uninterrupt-ed.

Dress comfortably in clothes suitable for the weather.

Find a peaceful, natural setting or a quiet, uncluttered indoor space if outdoor options are limited.

Centering and Grounding:

Stand or sit comfortably with your feet firmly planted on the ground.

Close your eyes, take several deep breaths, and visualize roots extend-ing from your body deep into the earth. Feel yourself grounded and con-nected to the earth's energy.

Opening the Circle:

If you are outdoors, physically walk in a clockwise circle to mark your sacred space. If indoors, you can imagine drawing a circle of light around you.

As you create the circle, say aloud or silently: "I cast this circle, a sacred space, to rewyld my spirit and reconnect with nature's grace."

Invocation of the Elements:

Stand facing the four cardinal directions (north, east, south, west).

Call upon the elements in each direction:

To the North, say: "Earth, stable and strong, grant me the grounding and resilience of the land."

To the East, say: "Air, swift and free, grant me the clarity and inspira-tion of the wind."

To the South, say: "Fire, passionate and transformative, grant me the courage and vitality of the flame."

To the West, say: "Water, fluid and emotional, grant me the intuition and adaptability of the river."

Affirmation and Intention:

Hold your journal and pen in your hands and set your intention for the ritual. What aspect of your spirit are you seeking to rewyld? Write it down as an affirmation.

For example: "I embrace the wild and untamed aspects of my spirit, reconnecting with nature and my inner instincts."

Nature Connection:

Spend some time in silence and observe the natural surroundings. Listen to the sounds of nature, feel the breeze or the earth beneath you, and connect with the living world around you.

Offer your small token or offering to nature as a symbol of your respect and gratitude.

Reflection and Journaling:

Sit quietly with your journal and pen and reflect on your intention. Write down any insights, thoughts, or emotions that arise during this time.

Closing the Circle:

Stand at the edge of your circle and thank the elements in each direction for their presence and energy.

Say aloud or silently: "I release this circle, but the connection remains within me."

Closing Words:

End the ritual with words of gratitude and affirmation. For example: "I am reconnected with the wild spirit within me and the natural world around me."

Release the Energy:

Now Dance, Move, Let your spirit soar. Let your inhibitions go and experience the wild energy around you. Feel your wild spirit take over and release all of the fear and need for control.

Integration:

Once you have exhausted yourself in the dance with nature, take your journal with you and continue to reflect on your experiences in the coming days. Embrace the wildness and untamed aspects of your spirit as you go about your daily life.

This ritual for rewylding the spirit is a personal journey of reconnecting with your primal nature and finding comfort and excitement in the untamed aspects of your soul. It can be repeated as often as needed to maintain that connection with the wild spirit within.

CHAPTER NINE
WYTCHCRAFT AND
ANIMAL FRIENDS—
THE WILDLINGS

"In the hush of dawn and the rustle of dusk, nature's wisdom speaks
softly, offering lessons carved by eons, reminding us that in its
embrace, we find the answers to the questions
the heart has yet to ask."

Let's talk about wytchcraft and how it involves working with animals and their surroundings. In many practices, there exists a profound connection between the wytch and nature's creatures. These companions are the ones I refer to as "The Wildlings." They aren't just ordinary animals; they are allies, sources of wisdom, and living manifestations of the world of magick. The relationship between a wytch and our animal friends is one of deep understanding that moves far beyond words. It's a connection of intuition and unspoken communication. Wytches often find that certain animals are drawn to them, or vice versa, and that these creatures become steadfast partners in our magickal journey.

The Wildlings are animals that you can find in nature– like birds, deer, or even your neighborhood raccoon. They are believed to be keepers of ancient wisdom and secrets of the natural world. I, personally, turn to these creatures to gain insights into my own craft, the cycles of nature, and hidden aspects of myself. Whether it's a crow with its sharp intelligence, a cat with its mysterious ways, or an opossum with its primal instincts, each animal brings its unique teachings to the wytch.

I personally believe that my affinity and connection toward certain animals is linked to my ancestral lineage. It's as if the spirits of my ancestors guide and work with me through these animal companions. The Wildlings serve as a bridge between present life and the wisdom of my ancestors, connecting me to certain traditions and energies that span generations. The Wildlings are not just spiritual guides; they offer emotional support and comfort in everyday life. A cat's purring, for example, can be soothing during meditation, while the presence of a dog can be grounding in times of stress. These allies become sources of strength, helping us to navigate the challenges of both the mundane and the mystical worlds.

The bond between me and The Wildlings is not one-sided. It's a relationship of mutual respect and care. I provide food, shelter, and love to my own animal companions and to my wilder allies while they offer guidance and companionship in return. It's an exchange that enriches both my life and theirs. The Wildlings are at the heart of my practice. They are a reminder to me of the connection between all beings and the importance of respecting and protecting the natural world. It's about living in harmony with the Earth and all its inhabitants.

To start bonding with the Wildlings, you don't need a secret spell. Just spend time outdoors and observe animals. It's like making friends – you get to know them and understand their world. Patience is the key here. I can't count the many afternoons and evenings that I have spent in the woods... just sitting. I use the time to ground and meditate, but I also use the time to nurture the relationships I have made with the creatures of those woods. I have found over the years that I am visited more by my animal friends when I go to the woods under cover of nightfall. During these quiet, peaceful times, I have encountered fox, raccoons, owls, and a critter that I have grown to have a love/hate relationship with...the southern opossum.

When I first started my nighttime rounds of the woods, I moved as silently as I could. I didn't make sudden movements or loud noises. In doing so, the animals didn't see me as a threat but as another woodland creature. I am always observing and always respectful. It is in these moments that I am able to learn nature's lessons.

The fox I have seen is constantly watching, ears pricked for any sound of an intruder. The opossum seems unworried about those around her and is only thinking of the next meal. Both creatures were very stand-offish at first but as they became accustomed to my treks into the woods, I found that they actually looked for me. It didn't hurt that I always brought offerings. I am very careful about 'treats' for wild animals. Any food offered is something that they would forage or find in the wild. I don't offer anything that could make them dependent on me or make them leave their wild ways in search of the life of a tamed pet.

In my wild encounters, I have had many of these feral yet tender creatures adopt me to some degree. The very first animal consort that I made acquaintance with was Mama Crow. To be honest, I've never known whether this crow was male or female but I felt protected and that she was watching over me with a maternal eye. She was always the one to alert me when someone or something was coming closer than she thought they should. I could visit the homes of friends, and she would fly over or alongside the car at a distance and then perch on top of their house or in their trees until it was time for me to leave. I had visited one friend who said that they had never seen a crow in their yard or close to their house until I came over for the first time. Mama Crow would make herself comfortable on the eave of the porch and make that loud, throaty caw. That sound came to represent protection and friendship to me. Even now, when I hear that rough, scratchy sound from crows in the area, it soothes me. I know that I will be ok.

Mama Crow has always been a generous soul. It hasn't been unusual over the years to find small gifts from her. I know they are from her because they have always been placed in the same spot or close to a place that she knows I will pass by. The normal gifts are typically coins, marbles (especially the big green glass ones), and even Christmas garland. I treasure these gifts and use them in my magick...especially protection magick.

An unexpected animal ally for me was the chipmunk. For a time, I lived in a small shack out behind some friend's home. Most afternoons and evenings were spent relaxing on the porch or reading on a stump or snacking as I watched the breeze dance through the treetops. It was during these moments of relaxation that I found two curious little chipmunks who were completely intrigued by the habits of this big, bald wytch. The first encounter was pretty common...I watched them dart back and forth around the foundation of the shack and over and around the stump.

It was a warm summer afternoon; I had decided to read propped up on the stump next to the shack. In the process, I dozed off with my arms crossed over the book on my chest. I woke up, and the sight that greeted me was sweet and shocking at the same time. I looked in the crook of my arm, and there was a chipmunk...sound asleep. In the short amount of time I had napped, it had decided that I looked like a comfortable alternative to the little space in the tree where they normally observed me.

My adventures with the chipmunks became the highlight of my days. If I brought a bag of chips or nuts outside with me, it was only a matter of time before I heard the crinkle of the wrapper and looked up to see a little chipmunk butt wiggling around inside the bag. They became adept at stealing my snacks and had no fear whatsoever around me. They became my friends and my guides at the same time. I learned much watching and interacting with them on a daily basis.

As fall approached, I built a fairy house to put acorns and nuts in to prepare them for the winter ahead. I would fill the little house up, and they would empty it. It was just as the final notes of fall played out that they disappeared. I know that they had begun the process of readying themselves and their nest for winter. Even though it brought a feeling of melancholy, I knew that this was just a normal part of their lifecycle and that they would be back in the spring. They were faithful to their nature. The next spring, I was greeted by not just two chipmunks, but by those two and their babies.

Not all of the animals I have worked with are, in my opinion, cute and cuddly. The old opossum who started coming around scared me to death just from looks alone, but I try not to be the type of person who would let their fear keep them from allowing an animal to become a friend.

I had just built a mini altar in the woods from a burned-out old tree stump. I had put leaves in the middle and stones around it. This way if I used candles or incense, it would contain the smoke or flame. One night, as I was sitting in front of the altar, I heard a noise coming from the right side of where I was sitting. It wasn't the sound of something moving fast and it sounded more like something taking a leisurely stroll rather than the sound of a predator in hunting mode. I breathed in deeply knowing that whatever it was going to either be a friend or something I didn't want to tangle with. I was right on both counts.

I looked over to my right side, and I saw glowing beady little eyes glinting in the candlelight. I knew what it was before my eyes even focused. I heard a disgruntled, slow hiss lurch from her mouth. She was old and tattered but with spunk. She stopped in her tracks far enough away that I didn't run screaming, and she didn't feel threatened. I spoke to her in soothing tones. She looked like she hadn't eaten in ages. I continued to talk to her, letting her know that I wasn't there to intrude or to hurt her. Was I scared out of my wits? Durn straight I was. Was I shaking from that fear? Durn straight I was. Did I let that keep me from interacting with this wobbling, ambling creature? I sure didn't. As I did my working at the altar, I talked and sang and moved slowly. She stayed put but watched every move I made. I knew in that moment that even though I was scared to death, that I had also begun cultivating a relationship with this old possum lady.

Each night that I would venture back into the woods would bring this gentle soul out of hiding. I decided then and there that she was a friend... no matter what she looked like. I have pet jumping spiders, so I always had grubworms, maggots, and roaches on hand for feedings. I gathered up a large bowl of those critters and dumped them on a leaf that I had made into a serving plate for her. She scarfed down each one with what I can only describe as elation. That toothy possum grin spread wide as she crunched down on the crunchy exterior of one of the cockroaches. With that one act of kindness, I now had another animal ally. She would slowly move closer to where I would sit whenever I was in the woods. In all honesty, I was a bit afraid to doze off. I couldn't take the thought of waking up to a possum cradled in the crook of my arm like the chipmunks had done, but if she did, then I would deal with it when it happened.

As I worked more with these animal allies, sometimes, these animals would show up in my dreams or in my thoughts. I am not one of those who 'does' Spirit Animals. I leave that to my indigenous friends. That is why I engage these animals as allies or as 'Wildlings.' Each one has its own magick and meanings associated with that magick. I look at dreams of certain animals with a more intuitive approach. If you dream of an owl, it might symbolize wisdom. A crow, to me, symbolizes a messenger of spirit and transformation. A fox symbolizes cunning and playfulness. Chipmunks represent laughter and a mischievous nature. An opossum symbolizes protection, problem-solving, and the ability to create illusion. We have something that we can learn from each creature, and in this communion, we are able to access magick that we may easily overlook in our day-to-day activities.

Having Wildling friends isn't just about observation and play. You can tap into their strengths and borrow a bit of their magick and energy. If you're friends with a squirrel, maybe you'll find yourself being more resourceful. If you make friends with a chipmunk, maybe you need more joy in your life. A possum can teach us to be more methodical and how to protect ourselves from those who may not have our best interests at heart.

In some traditions, a Wildling can become your "familiar." Think of them as your sidekick. They can help boost your own magick and show you bits of wisdom. Wildlings are built for survival and own a magick that we, as humans, may easily overlook as unnecessary or old fashioned. These creatures hold a magick that is older than the woods itself. It is born into them. Unlike humans, they don't think or reason away those parts of themselves.

Now, here's the important part. Wytchcraft with the Wildlings isn't about taking from nature. Wytches who work with these animal allies know it's crucial to treat them and their homes with care and respect. Wytchcraft and the Wildlings are all about connecting with nature and the animals around us. It's making friends and learning from them. Just remember to be a responsible friend and ally and take care of their environment.

Exercise: "Discovering Your Animal Allies"

Objective: This exercise guides you in exploring and connecting with animal energies and symbolism to discover potential animal allies that resonate with your inner self.

Instructions:

1. Quiet and Reflective Space:

Find a quiet and comfortable space where you can focus inward without distractions.

2. Journal or Notebook:

Have a journal or notebook and a pen ready to record your thoughts and observations.

3. Set Your Intentions:

Begin by setting your intention for this exercise: to discover and connect with animal energies that can offer guidance and support in your life.

4. Inner Exploration:

Close your eyes and take a few deep breaths to center yourself. Imagine entering a serene and peaceful forest in your mind's eye.

5. Meeting Place:

In your forest visualization, envision a clearing where you feel safe and at ease. Imagine this as a place where you can meet and commune with animal energies.

6. Call to the Animal Allies:

In your visualization, invite the presence of animal allies. Silently or aloud, ask for their guidance, wisdom, and protection.

7. Observe and Interact:

Pay attention to any animals that appear in your mental landscape. These may be real animals or fantastical creatures. Observe their behaviors, appearances, and any messages they convey.

8. Journal Reflection:

Open your eyes and return to your physical space. Immediately write down your experiences in your journal. Describe the animals you encountered and the feelings or insights you received.

9. Symbolism Research:

Research the symbolism and meanings associated with the animals you encountered. Books, online resources, and reputable websites can provide valuable information.

10. Personal Connection:

Reflect on how the symbolism and characteristics of these animals resonate with your own life and personality. Consider the challenges, strengths, or guidance they might offer.

11. Choose Animal Allies:

Based on your experiences and research, choose one or more animal allies that deeply resonate with you. These are the animals you feel a strong connection to and wish to invite into your life as guides.

12. Symbolic Representation:

Find or create a symbolic representation of your chosen animal allies. This could be an image, a figurine, or any meaningful representation that serves as a reminder of their presence in your life.

13. Integration:

Incorporate the energy and symbolism of your animal allies into your daily life. You can do this by meditating with their representation, carrying it with you, or setting up a dedicated altar.

14. Gratitude:

Express gratitude to your chosen animal allies for their presence and guidance. Regularly take a moment to acknowledge their support in your life.

15. Ongoing Connection:

Continue to explore and deepen your connection with your animal allies over time. They can provide valuable insights and support in various aspects of your life.

Let's Do the Working:

Ritual of Embracing the Wildlings

This ritual is designed to forge a deeper connection with your animal allies, also known as "The Wildlings," and seek their guidance and wisdom in your magickal practice.

Materials:
- A quiet, natural setting (outdoors or a room with plants)
- A small offering, such as birdseed or nuts
- A candle (color of your choice...I use brown or green to represent

nature)

– A quiet and open heart

Preparation:

1. Find a serene and natural setting, preferably where you can feel the presence of wildlife or you can use house plants if you're indoors.

2. Place the candle at the center of your chosen space.

3. Light the candle, and as the flame flickers to life, take a few deep breaths to center yourself.

Ritual Steps:

1. Grounding and Centering:

Stand or sit comfortably, feeling the energy of the earth beneath you.

Close your eyes and imagine roots extending from your body into the ground, anchoring you to the Earth.

2. Invocation:

Open your eyes and light the candle.

Say aloud or in your mind: "I call upon the spirits of the Wildlings, my animal allies, to join me in this sacred space. Be with me as I seek your wisdom and guidance."

3. Offering:

Place the offering (birdseed or nuts) beside the candle.

Express gratitude for the animals and their guidance in your life.

4. Silent Connection:

Sit in quiet contemplation, focusing on your breath.

Imagine the animals you feel a connection with coming near. Observe them in your mind's eye, and allow their presence to wash over you.

5. Speak Your Intent:

When you feel the presence of your animal allies, speak your intent aloud or in your mind. For example: "I seek your wisdom, dear Wildlings.

Help me understand [your specific question or intention]."

I use a song that I wrote a few years ago as my intent:

In the whispering woods, under the moon's soft gleam,
The Wildlings gather, like a mystical dream.
With fur and feathers, and eyes so wise,
They dance in moonlight, beneath starlit skies.

(Chorus)
Oh, Wildlings, you're magick in fur and in flight,
Guiding our spirits through day and through night.
With whispers of secrets, in nature's embrace,
We sing to you now, in this sacred space.

In the rustling leaves and the rivers that flow,
You teach us the secrets that only you know.
With paws on the earth and wings on the breeze,
You lead us to places where our spirits find ease.

(Chorus)
Oh, Wildlings, you're magick in fur and in flight,
Guiding our spirits through day and through night.
With whispers of secrets, in nature's embrace,
We sing to you now, in this sacred space.

(Bridge)
Through forests and meadows, where mysteries lie,
You're our companions, our spirits ally.
In unity with nature, we find our delight,
With the Wildlings beside us, our hearts take to flight.

(Chorus)

Oh, Wildlings, you're magick in fur and in flight,
Guiding our spirits through day and through night.
With whispers of secrets, in nature's embrace,
We sing to you now, in this sacred space.

(Outro)

As the moonlight fades and the stars softly wane,
We thank you, dear Wildlings, for sharing your reign.
In the heart of the wild, where dreams take their flight,
We'll forever sing to you, in the cool of the night.

6. Listen and Observe:

Keep your mind open and receptive. Pay attention to any thoughts, images, or feelings that arise.

Take note of any animals that may appear in your surroundings, either physically or in your mind's eye.

7. Gratitude and Farewell:

Thank your animal allies for their presence and guidance.

Blow out the candle, symbolizing the end of the ritual.

8. Reflect and Record:

Spend some time reflecting on your experience and record it in your journal or Book of Shadows or Grimoire.

Pay attention to any animal encounters or signs in the days following the ritual, as they may hold further guidance.

Conclusion:

This ritual serves as a bridge to the world of animal allies, The Wildlings, inviting their wisdom and guidance into your magickal practice. As you continue your journey in wytchcraft, remember to nurture and honor this connection, as it can offer profound insights and strengthen your bond with the natural world.

CHAPTER TEN
LEARNING THE LANGUAGE
OF THE FOREST

"When the forest calls your name, Nature is beckoning you to escape
the chaos of daily life and step into its tranquil sanctuary. It's an
invitation to leave behind the noise of the world and embrace the
sounds of bird songs and rustling leaves. The trees stand as ancient
watchmen, their branches like open arms ready to cradle your
worries. In the heart of the forest, you can rediscover a connection to
something greater, something timeless, and find a sense of peace that
soothes your spirit and renews your soul."

In the world of witchcraft, there exists a hidden language—one spoken not
with words but with the rustle of leaves, the rush of river water, and the
whispers of ancient trees. It is the language of the forest. This language
is known to those who walk the path of any nature-based magick. In this
chapter, we will dive head-first into the art of learning and understanding
this mystical tongue.

To begin your journey into the language of the forest, you must first
learn to listen. The forest has a silent song that carries messages in the
wind and in the echoes of footsteps on its leafy floor. I find that I hear this
message best when I sit beneath a an old oak or beside a river or pond. If
I close my eyes and let nature's melody envelop me, each breath tunes in to
the forest's heartbeat and pulses in time with the earth itself.

This language is not a language of humans but of the spirits that live there. To understand this language, you must form a connection with these spirits. Offerings of gratitude: I have personally used handfuls of dried herbs, a sprinkle of fresh water, or even a purposefully placed crystal. I always approach with respect and humility, for the forest's spirits are old and wise.

Within the forest, you will find symbols and signs that speak of magick. The shape of a leaf, the arrangement of stones, or the sound of a bird— these are all part of the forest's song. I have learned with many years of practice to learn to decipher these symbols by building relationships with the forest and its spirits.

Plants are some of the most eloquent speakers in the forest's language. They offer their wisdom in the form of herbal remedies, spells, and potions. I have studied the plants in local to my area and learned what they can do. I have found that working closely with nature will offer guidance when I need it.

As I have partnered with nature, I have found that the first step is to establish a sacred grove—a place of power where the forest's energy unites. In the space that I have created, I perform rituals and spells and commune with nature to deepen the connection. It is within these spaces that the forest's voice is most clear to me.

The trees themselves have been great teachers. I love to spend time in their presence, touch their bark, and listen to their stories. I often take naps under the trees and when I dream, I ask for the guidance of the tree spirits. In my own personal experience, their messages often come in the form of vivid dreams or whispered secrets.

Along that same vein, the wind carries messages across the forest. To understand its whispers, you must become attuned to its subtleties. During meditation, I invite the wind to share its wisdom with me. I don't just listen with my ears, but I have learned to listen and feel with my entire being. The most powerful magick I have ever experienced is dancing with the wind. In those dances, I have found that I am able to shake off the cares of the world and feel the freedom that only comes as an unfettered dance partner to a breeze.

Lastly, remember that the most profound messages from the forest often come in the form of silence. In moments of stillness, I have found some of the deepest insights that the forest can share. In these moments of quiet, I am more attuned to the voice of spirit. It is within the whispers that I am able to calmly focus on the things that the hurried world around me would rather I forget or overlook.

In the language of the forest, there are no dictionaries or textbooks. It is a language of intuition, feeling, and connection. The forest is a patient entity, and it, in turn, has taught me patience and strength.

Through the years, I have become close friends with the forest. I have learned many lessons and have enjoyed the beauty and the calm that it rewards me as a steward. My own 'sacred grove' is an old burned-out tree stump. It lies yards away from the biggest oak tree I have ever seen. This oak tree has seen so many of my own emotions and offered comfort when I needed it. It has seen all of my magick and lent itself to those workings. It has nurtured all manner of wildings and has been a warrior for me in my own journey. I have traveled and worked in many forests in my years and have found that the energies of each must speak to the other. I have never once not felt at home among the trees and animals whether in North Carolina, Tennessee, or Georgia.

The woods have always been a second home for me. There have been many a lunchtime visit to help me separate myself from the corporate world. Working from home has allowed me the option of putting my feet in the dirt and napping under an old tree during my lunch hour. It keeps me sane through the troubles that everyday life throws my way.

Yesterday, I was dealing with a bit of a headache so I decided to go spend some time in the woods. I walked slowly, trying not to disturb any spiderwebs dancing amongst the lower branches of the trees. As I shifted my body to avoid a beautiful orb weaver spider who had been carefully spinning its web, I chuckled to myself, thinking of MawMaw's old warning. Be careful of those old orb weavers. If they write your name in their web, you're going to die before the next full moon.

I rounded the old pine trees and looked for my favorite oak. As I settled against it, I could feel my body sink into the peace that only moss and lichen and the leaves on the forest floor can offer. As I sat sleepily next to the oak, I looked up and saw what seemed like hundreds of dragonflies playing on the breeze. In that moment, you just know that you are home and that the troubles that were coming at you when you got there were going to be soon gone.

Learning the language of the woods is like anything else. It has to be nurtured, practiced, and fully experienced. It is a relationship, and like all relationships, time is the key.

When the forest calls your name, Nature is beckoning you to escape the chaos of everyday life and step into its tranquil sanctuary. It's an invitation to leave behind the noise of the world and embrace the sounds of bird songs and rustling leaves. The trees stand as ancient watchmen, their branches like open arms ready to cradle your worries. In the heart of the forest, you can rediscover a connection to something so much greater, something timeless, and find a sense of peace that soothes your spirit and renews your soul.

Exercise: "Listening to the Language of the Forest"

Objective: This exercise encourages you to connect with the natural world and develop a deeper understanding of the subtle language spoken by the forest.

Instructions:

1. Forest Immersion:

Find a quiet and secluded spot in a forest, woodland, or any natural area with trees. If you're unable to access a physical forest, a peaceful park or wooded area will suffice.

2. Digital Detox:

Disconnect from electronic devices. Leave your phone, tablet, or any distractions behind. This exercise is about immersing yourself in nature without technological interference.

3. Mindful Arrival:

As you enter the forest or wooded area, take a moment to stand still. Close your eyes, take a few deep breaths, and consciously transition from the busyness of everyday life to the tranquility of the forest.

4. Forest Sit:

Find a comfortable spot to sit or lean against a tree. Choose a place where you can be still and observe your surroundings.

5. The Five Senses:

Engage your senses fully. Close your eyes and listen to the sounds around you—the rustling leaves, birdsong, or the gentle breeze. Touch the earth beneath your fingers and notice its texture. Inhale deeply and savor the scents of the forest. Open your eyes and observe the colors, shapes, and details of the trees and flora. If safe, taste a wild edible plant or simply taste the air.

6. Soundscape Awareness:

Pay particular attention to the sounds of the forest. Focus on individual sounds, such as the chirping of birds, the flow of water, or the rustling of leaves. Let the forest's auditory tapestry wash over you.

7. Tree Connection:

Choose one tree to focus on. It could be an old, wise tree that calls to you or simply the one closest to your sitting spot. Observe its bark, branches, and leaves. Feel a connection to its presence.

8. Forest Communication:

In your journal or simply in your thoughts, write down any sensations, emotions, or messages you receive from the forest. Consider what it might be saying to you, even if it's not in words.

9. Silent Contemplation:

Spend time in silent contemplation, allowing the forest to communicate with you on a deep, intuitive level. Trust your instincts and intuition as you connect with the natural world.

10. Journal Reflection:

Open your eyes and return to your physical surroundings. In your journal, record your experiences, thoughts, and any insights gained during your forest immersion.

11. Regular Practice:

Commit to regularly practicing this exercise, visiting the forest or natural area whenever you can. Each visit may bring new insights and connections.

12. Gratitude:

Express gratitude to the forest for allowing you to listen to its language and for the wisdom it imparts. Recognize the interconnectedness of all living beings.

Let's Do the Working:

Ritual: Learning the Language of the Forest

Intention: This ritual is designed to help you connect with the natural world and begin to learn the language of the forest, a symbolic and intuitive form of communication with nature.

Items Needed:
  – A quiet, natural setting (a forest, woodland, or secluded park)
  – Comfortable clothing suitable for spending time outdoors

– A journal or notebook

– A pen or pencil

– A small offering (such as a handful of birdseed, a flower, or a piece of fruit)

– An open heart and a sense of wonder

Procedure:

1. Choose Your Sacred Space:

Find a quiet, secluded spot in a natural setting like a forest or woodland. Ensure that you won't be disturbed during your ritual.

2. Cleansing and Grounding:

Stand quietly in your chosen spot and take several deep breaths. Close your eyes and visualize any tension or distractions leaving your body and being absorbed by the earth beneath you.

3. Offering to the Spirits:

Hold your small offering in your hand and say a simple, heartfelt prayer or affirmation. Express your gratitude and intention to connect with the forest and its inhabitants. Place the offering on the ground as a gift.

4. Meditative Walk:

Begin to walk slowly and mindfully through the forest. Pay close attention to the sights, sounds, and sensations around you. Feel the earth beneath your feet and the rhythm of your breath.

5. Silent Observation:

Find a comfortable spot to sit or stand. Close your eyes and listen. Observe the sounds of the forest—the rustling leaves, chirping birds, and flowing water. Try to discern patterns and meanings in the sounds.

6. Nature Journaling:

Open your journal or notebook and start to write or sketch what you observe and feel. Describe the colors, shapes, and textures of the plants and trees. Record any thoughts or impressions that come to you.

7. Engage Your Senses:

Take the time to touch the leaves, smell the earth, and feel the texture of the bark. Engage all your senses to deepen your connection with the forest.

8. Meditation and Intuition:

Close your eyes and enter a meditative state. Visualize yourself communicating with the forest. Ask for guidance, wisdom, or any messages that nature may offer. Be open to intuitive insights.

9. Symbolic Connection:

Choose a particular tree, plant, or natural feature that resonates with you. Approach it and gently touch or hug it as a symbolic act of connection. Feel the energy exchange between you and this natural element.

10. Gratitude and Farewell:

As your ritual comes to a close, express your gratitude to the forest and its spirits for welcoming you. Promise to return and continue learning their language.

11. Journal Reflection:

Sit once more with your journal and record your experiences, insights, and any messages you received during the ritual. Reflect on what you've learned and how you can continue to deepen your connection with the forest.

12. Closing the Ritual:

Stand and thank the forest one final time. Leave your offering to the spirits and walk slowly back to your starting point, feeling the profound connection you've cultivated.

This ritual is a starting point for learning the language of the forest, which is a deeply personal and intuitive practice. Each time you visit the woods, you'll become more attuned to its language, and the wisdom of the natural world will continue to unfold before you.

CHAPTER ELEVEN
THE GREEN WIZARD

"In our everyday lives, the heart often yearns for something more,
something beyond the ordinary. It craves a touch of magick, the
kind that makes the world feel a bit brighter and more captivating,
It's in the simple moments, like a sunset's warm glow or the laughter
of loved ones, that we find the magick our hearts seek. So, embrace
those moments, for the heart craves magick in the every day, and
it's often right there, waiting to be discovered in the beauty of life's
simple pleasures."

It seemed, when I was small, that I constantly got into trouble for who I
talked to. The words meander through my brain now as I write...my Pop
would always warn me, "Don't spend your time talking out loud to animals
when we are out. People will think you're odd." I never had a sense of not
being able to or not wanting to talk to animals or anyone else for that matter...they always talked back to me.

As I mentioned earlier, our town was home to 'Crazy Mary.' She wandered the streets of my hometown dressed in every stitch of clothes that
she owned with a shopping cart she had 'borrowed' from Gamble's grocery. She was always kept in supply, by that same grocer, of the one snack
that she adored...mustard-covered sardines. Ma told me a few years back
that my dad had taken me downtown (twenty or so stores and a court-
house) one Saturday. We were walking down the sidewalk, and my dad
ran into an old friend of the family. After their conversation, they looked

around for me, and I was nowhere to be found. They finally found me sitting on the covered stoop next to the old Center movie theater, laughing out loud and sharing a tin of mustard-covered sardines with 'Crazy Mary.' I was probably five...I knew no fear then, but in later years, I was taught to fear her just because she was different.

That is where my heart for abandoned people and animals started. I have never understood categorizing someone or something as having no worth. Surely, there was something important enough about the essence of the spirit that caused that person or animal to come into being. As I have mentioned before, I am scared to death of an opossum, but that doesn't mean it has no purpose.

I can remember a Monday several years ago, just like it was yesterday. It was a beautiful spring-like evening here in Atlanta. I had come home to the roomie having every window open, and the inside of the house smelled fresh...like the cave-like conditions of winter had been pushed out the windows. The plague of 'green snow' (pollen for you non-natives) had not fully hit, so it seemed like a good evening to take Friz, my little blue chihuahua, for a walk. Frisbee was my magickal ally if I ever had one. He was always right in the middle of where the magick happened. He was given to me for my birthday, and he never left my side until the day he moved from this realm to the next.

We walked our usual path toward the woods. It seemed like the perfect evening to just lie down under the canopy of branches and leaves that the woods had erupted into overnight. I talked to Friz every step of the way, and he listened intently. As we rounded one of the corners of our condominium complex over close to where we scoot off the pathway, I looked up, and sitting on a column of bricks was a young man of about 28 or so with a medium-sized mutt at his feet. He was dressed in a brown shirt with brown pants and a green hooded cloak. Everything he wore had a patina to it...you could tell that they had been well-worn. As I stood there looking him over from head to toe, I noticed that the shoes he wore were black converse that had seen better days. The soles were falling off and you could see the dirty socks inside.

I trust my dog completely when it comes to the nature of other people and animals, so I looked down at Friz to see if he was giving me any sign of alert. He looked straight at the young man and his dog with his tongue out and his tail wagging...so I took this as my cue to move forward.

As we moved closer, the young man looked up at me underneath the hood and spoke softly, "She won't bite. She is really gentle." We moved even closer. Friz initiated the dog handshake, and after they had both gotten a nostril full, Friz licked the gentle dog on her muzzle. The docile animal turned to Friz and only licked back. I leaned over and gave the dog a scratch behind the ear, and she leaned in sweetly. The young man pulled the hood away from his face and introduced himself to me. "They call me the Green Wizard, and this is my dog Calliope." I weighed the situation cautiously at first. "They call me the Weathered Wiseman, and this is Friz." He leaned into Friz to give him a scratch under his chin, and Friz licked the calloused hand, making its way toward him.

The 'Green Wizard' looked up at me and smiled as wide as his mouth allowed. "There's gotta be something said for the wizard's dog." He laughed out loud as his dog and Friz played and eventually rolled over on top of each other. As we sat there talking, he told me stories of his travels...how he prefers to sleep out among the grass and trees, under the moon and stars. He told me about the animals that work their magick around him and the importance of seeing magick in everything that makes its way to us. I watched as his eyes twinkled, and he seemed to exude something akin to what I would think fairy magick would hold.

Was everything he told me true? I don't know. Was he who he said he was? Again, I don't know. My dog liked him. His dog liked me....and honestly, he could ask himself those same questions about me. The only thing I knew for certain at that time was that I was able to spend a couple of hours talking to someone fascinating...someone who held a magick within himself whether I or anyone else around believed it. The magick within him resonated something strong within my own spirit. Whether this was a truth that the world would believe, maybe not, but this was his truth…and for a brief moment, I was allowed to share it.

I only know what my heart felt like that evening. My heart felt completely alive in those couple of hours. It was as if the heartbeat of the Earth sang in my own chest. Was the interaction between him and me dangerous? I trust my dog…and I trust what is inside of me. I know if there had been something off, my own spirit would have kicked into overdrive, and our conversation would have never started.

As we finished talking, I looked down at his shoes. Those shoes had seen so much travel. I remembered that I always kept an extra pair of shoes in my car, and our feet looked to be about the same size. I asked if he would be there for a few more minutes. He told me he would, so Friz and I sprinted to the back of the complex to my car. I pulled out a pair of athletic shoes that hadn't been worn much…but they were about to embark on a journey that could not even be fathomed.

Friz and I walked back to that brick column, and I handed him the shoes. I told him that I wanted to give him something that would help his journey. He thanked me with a hug and asked if he might 'give me a blessing.' I told him that the time I had spent with him that afternoon was blessing enough. I bid him peace and safe travels. Friz and I stood there as the moon began to rise. We watched the Green Wizard walk toward the glow of the moon. That young man may never have another occasion to remember me, but he is etched into every corner of my mind and a place in my heart that I didn't know existed.

As I look back on my times with the Green Wizard, I can see how everything in life orders itself. It was early one morning, Friz and I decided to walk a path that we haven't traveled in a while. We headed out toward the pond, and as we got closer, Friz's tail started rotating wildly. If he could have picked up enough momentum, I believe he would have left the ground. I looked up and in the distance saw a familiar mutt loping toward us. Friz couldn't stand it...he wanted to play. I have to admit, too, that my heart skipped a beat or two in excitement. I questioningly called out, "Calliope?" The dog's tongue lolled out of her mouth, and she ran harder toward us. When she reached us, she danced around my legs, and Friz danced along with her.

We walked along the path that had been created by so many of my and Friz's journeys before. As we arrived at the edge of the pond, we moved closer to the trees that dotted the landscape. Leaning against the one that Friz and I normally shared, was the Green Wizard. He was reaching into his pocket, pulling out handfuls of something, and throwing it toward a murder of crows scavenging the grass. As I got closer, he stopped what he was doing and stood to his feet. A smile came to his face as he said, "Good morning, Weathered Wiseman." I smiled and chuckled, "Good morning, Green Wizard."

We both sat down in the grass....the talk came so easy...as if we had known each other for centuries. We talked of the coming Blood Moon and the energy that would be available at that time. We talked about the closeness of Beltane and our mutual love for the sleek black gravelly voiced birds that surrounded us. We laughed and talked about our love for the fur people and feathered ones and any other manner of critter.

I asked him what he had been feeding the crows. He pulled his hand out of his pocket and opened it to reveal kernels of corn spilling out. I asked him where he had gotten it and he told me that there was a huge pile of it under a few trees a ways back....then I remembered the neighbor who likes to feed the squirrels. More than once, I have seen Friz look up at me with the remnants of birdseed and corn around his mouth from foraging and finding her huge piles of squirrel food....and of course, the large amounts of poop that followed. I was amazed at the number of crows within walking distance of us that morning. They were having the most wonderful time. They were cawing back and forth...moving non-stop.

The Green Wizard turned to me again and, with a more-than-serious face, asked, "Why aren't you afraid of me? Why don't you rush in another direction when you see me...the way your neighbors do?" I answered truthfully, "I am not threatened by you. I see nothing to fear. I feel a kinship....and my dog likes you." Right then, as if on cue, Friz stretches and pushes his back feet against the Green Wizard. He laughed and told me that the reason he trusted me was also because his dog liked me. I was actually able to look into his eyes at that moment. There, staring back at me through the damage inflicted by the elements, was a softness. Such kindness and truth like I had never seen; he looked right into my spirit. I don't offer that type of vulnerability usually without trust being proven.

He smiled and said, "Weathered Wiseman, the coming moon brings so much to you. You need to take your time with her. Woo her. Sit with her and talk to her. She is the key to all that you have set into motion." I sat there with my mouth gaped open. I am amazed that such wisdom comes out of someone so young. I am then reminded that even though he is young, he has been seasoned well by wind, water, earth, and the fire of the sun and by the breath of spirit.

It was then that he said something to me that I knew beyond knowing. He told me that we had known each other in other lives. We had been connected many times before, and we would be connected many times more. I know where the connection lies, and I feel he does too, but we quietly sit and enjoy the sounds of the dogs snoring and grunting. He leans his head back to rest, and I do the same. All I can think is that this is a man who seems to have nothing other than his dog....but yet, not once has he ever asked me for anything. I get up and tell him that Friz and I will be right back. I go to the condo and make an egg and cheese sandwich with a travel mug of milk. I bag up a big portion of Friz's kibble for Calliope.

I walk back down to the pond, and he is standing up. I hand him the sandwich and he thanks me. He eats it slowly....savoring every bite. The reaction I didn't expect was the one I got when I handed him the dog food. He choked on the words as he thanked me and scooped his hand into the bag. He talked to Calliope sweetly and tenderly as he fed her from his hand. She, too, seemed to savor every bite.

We said our goodbyes. I never knew if it would be the last time we would see each other or whether I would see him again the next week. All I know is that I have learned valuable lessons in perception from this magickal young man.

Never look at anything the way those around you expect you to. Always look upon someone or something with a heart of magick, vulnerability, truth and love. It is in those moments that you will see that person or thing for what it truly is. On that day, if only for a moment, I was suspended in a realm of magick I had felt many times but not quite as intensely as I did that day. I had very possibly spent time with the greatest wizard in the world. He lived his life simply and with great humility and love. I had witnessed some of the most powerful magick that would ever exist.

There were many more encounters with the Green Wizard, but one last memory stands out in my mind. I was walking Friz through the complex one morning. Again, we were greeted by the sight of a dusty green cloak and a familiar mop of dirty brown hair. He sat in the same spot he was for our other visits. It tore at my heart to see him sitting alone. Isn't that how most of us try to face the challenges and hurts in our lives, though? Alone. There was no sweet old pup with her tongue lolling out to the side. His face lit up when he saw little Friz saunter up to him. Friz's whole body shook with joy, seeing our friend against the early morning darkness. The green wizard scooped him up and leaned into the thousands of licks that invaded his cheeks.

We walked and talked as he carried Friz close to his chest. I asked him where Calliope was…secretly knowing what he would say. He talked about how hard the past week had been for him.…like a part of his heart had been ripped out. He said that it felt like walking with one leg and no staff. Sleeping was hard because he had always fallen asleep listening to

Calliope breathing. I looked in his eyes and noticed that the sparkle that is normally visible was faint. His eyes looked weak. As we moved closer to the center of the woods, he seemed relieved to see the canape of branches and leaves above us. He lay down in the midst of the leaves and pine needles. Friz took the opportunity to crawl up onto his belly and settle in.

I never knew how often the green wizard got to eat, so that morning, I had made a cottage cheese carton full of grits and eggs and cheese. I handed it to him with a bottle of juice. He laughed out loud, "Who would have ever thought that I would have run into another magickal being here in the middle of this condominium complex...much less two?" I saw him wink at Friz as he said it. He ate slowly....savoring every bite. He shared a bite with Friz here and there. We talked about magick. We talked about animals. We talked about friendships. We laughed about unlikely friendships. I sat there as he rode the winds of his own storm. I watched as he released the pain of loss.

It amazes me how much magick is contained in the things that we seem to take for granted. The wytches of old knew this. Most of their magick involved the things found in everyday life. Herbs, animals...the things that were right outside their doors. Who would know that tears could be such a powerful potion. It is this magick that stirs inside of us that can bring healing, peace of mind, understanding and courage.

I was taken back to my childhood today. I have written about Crazy Mary...the local homeless person in my hometown. Everyone was afraid of her...they always went the other way. I remember her smile as a five-year-old hugged her. That memory washed over me today. As I wrapped my arms around the green wizard, I could feel the magick working. How many had turned the other way when they saw him? How many had kept from making eye contact? He had his own troubles to work through, just like everyone else.

My last encounter with the Green Wizard is forever etched in my memory. Friz and I rounded our usual corner...that same one that we always look toward with anticipation. We weren't disappointed. There perched the Green Wizard, but at the bottom part of the column was a lump of hair. I strained my eyes to get a better look. As we got closer, Friz went into his little general pose. His tail went straight up, and he began to make the sound of a low siren in his chest that generated a loud wail. There was a dog with the Green Wizard. As I got closer, I could see that it was some type of herding dog mix. It was a good looking dog...but how did it come to be with the Green Wizard?

When I got close enough to both of them, I could see the immense grin on the Green Wizard's face. By now, Friz was calming down a bit, and the sniffing had started. There were no growls...just tons of sniffing and butt-wagging. I asked the Green Wizard, "Where did you get him/her?" "He is a him, but he has been neutered. I was walking in the outskirts of the city, and on a not-so-busy street, a car drove by, and I watched as he was pushed out of the door as the car slowed down. He chased the car for a bit but finally gave up. I walked toward him and held my hand out. He looked as if he had just lost everything...so I asked him if he wanted to go with me... and here we are." Unfortunately, one thing I have seen in Atlanta is that some animals, as well as some people, are looked at as disposable.

I was totally amazed at the story. I could see a few abrasions on the dog. He seemed to have good teeth and strong muscles. He was probably only about a year old. He had the shape of a Border Collie, Shepherd... who knows what mix. He was probably way too much energy for the people who abandoned him.

We walked on toward the woods. I asked the Green Wizard if he had named his new friend. "His name is Boomer. That's short for Boomerang." He winked at me as he said this. I had told him the story of wanting to name our other dog Boomerang so that we would have a Frisbee and a Boomerang in our care. So here we walk toward the woods...a Weathered Wiseman, a Green Wizard, a Frisbee, and a Boomerang.

Friz is a great judge of character...I guess he figured that since this new dog was a friend to the Green Wizard that he might as well play nice. We settled down in our clearing. Boomer nestled in closely to the Green Wizard…he put his head down on his leg. I can imagine that he longed for that contact…that certainty that he wouldn't be deserted again. The Green Wizard leaned down and kissed him on the top of the head.

As I set up an altar…candles, skulls, crystals…I would lean in to light the candles. I will say that Boomer was a curious pup. He would lean in close to the candle, where I guess the smoke tickled his nose. He would huff and blow the candle out. We went through this process at least three times. It was a night of animal magick. I performed Reiki on Boomer as Friz wallowed in the lap of the Green Wizard. When I finished, it was like having a wobbly, putty-like dog in my hands. He ambled back over to the Green Wizard. I watched as they put nose to nose, forehead to forehead. I listened as the Green Wizard whispered to his new companion that he would never have to worry about being left or abandoned again. I watched as this dog leaned his weight into this young man, choosing to believe every word he said. He chose to cling to his new beginning.

I whispered blessings over my friend and his new companion. I watched as they both drifted off to sleep under the night sky. I packed up and asked him if he wanted to come with me. He followed me through the complex. I had not even paid attention to the fact that Boomer was wearing the collar that Calliope had worn. As we said our goodbyes, I watched as a soul steeped in so much magick and compassion spoke calming and loving words to another soul who had been left on his own by society as well. Magick is not a respecter of persons. It doesn't require wealth or knowledge or status…it only requires desire and passion. Once you combine those things with intent, the magick does the rest.

Exercise: "Seeing Others with Open Eyes"

Objective: This exercise encourages you to practice seeing and understanding others without pre-judgment, allowing for more compassionate and empathetic interactions.

Instructions:

1. Reflection Time:

    Find a quiet and comfortable space where you can sit and reflect without distractions.

2. Journal or Notebook:

    Have a journal or notebook and a pen ready to record your thoughts and observations.

3. Setting Intentions:

    Start by setting your intention for this exercise: to become more aware of your pre-judgments and to practice seeing others with fresh eyes and an open heart.

4. Self-Reflection:

    Begin by reflecting on your own biases, preconceptions, and judgments. Consider any stereotypes or assumptions you might carry about certain groups of people or individuals.

5. Identifying Pre-Judgments:

    In your journal, make a list of any common pre-judgments or stereotypes you are aware of. These could be related to factors like appearance, race, gender, age, or background.

6. Mindful Observation:

    In your daily life, practice mindful observation of people you encounter. This could be in public spaces, at work, or in social situations.

7. Suspension of Judgment:

    Whenever you catch yourself making a pre-judgment about someone, consciously pause. Instead of reacting based on that judgment, remind yourself that you don't know their full story.

8. Curiosity and Empathy:

Shift your perspective by asking questions in your mind. What might be their experiences, struggles, or joys? Imagine what life might be like from their point of view.

9. Avoid Assumptions:

Make a conscious effort to avoid making assumptions about people based on limited information. Recognize that each person is complex and unique.

10. Empathetic Listening:

When you engage in conversations with others, practice empathetic listening. Give them your full attention and try to understand their feelings, thoughts, and perspectives without judgment.

11. Journal Reflection:

At the end of each day, reflect on your experiences. Write in your journal about any instances where you successfully suspended judgment and saw someone with fresh eyes.

12. Self-Compassion:

Be gentle with yourself throughout this process. Acknowledge that challenging and changing pre-judgments is an ongoing practice.

13. Share and Discuss:

If you feel comfortable, discuss your experiences and insights with a friend, family member, or support group. Sharing your journey can deepen your understanding and commitment to seeing others without pre-judgment.

14. Continued Practice:

Commit to making this exercise a regular part of your life. Over time, it can lead to more open and empathetic interactions with people from all walks of life.

15. Gratitude:

Express gratitude for the opportunities to grow and learn through seeing others without pre-judgment. Recognize the beauty in embracing diversity and the richness of human experiences.

Let's Do the Working:

Ritual: Looking past the exterior

Items Needed:
  – A quiet, sacred space where you won't be disturbed.
  – A white candle (for clarity and insight).
  – A lighter or matches.
  – A small bowl of water.
  – A piece of clear quartz crystal (for clarity and amplifying energy).
  – A small mirror or reflective surface.
  – Incense (optional, for purification. I use rosemary and dragon's blood resin).
  – A journal and a pen.

Steps:
  1. Preparation: Find or create a quiet, sacred space where you can sit or stand comfortably. Clear the space of any distractions and clutter.
  2. Cleansing (optional):Light the incense and pass it around your body and the ritual space to purify the energy. As you do this, visualize any negative or stagnant energy dissipating.
  3. Light the Candle: Light the white candle and place it in front of you. As you do this, set your intention for the ritual: to see beyond the surface, gain insight, and understand things and people on a deeper level.
  4. Connect with Water: Dip your fingertips into the bowl of water. As you do, say, "By the element of water, I cleanse my perception and open my inner sight."

5. Hold the Crystal: Take the clear quartz crystal in your hand and close your eyes. Imagine a bright, white light surrounding you, cleansing and purifying your energy. Feel this light flowing through you, dispelling any mental clutter or distractions.

6. Gazing Meditation: Place the small mirror or reflective surface in front of the candle. Gaze into the mirror, allowing your mind to relax. Don't force anything; simply observe any thoughts, images, or feelings that arise.

7. Affirmation: While gazing into the mirror, repeat an affirmation, such as, "I see beyond the surface, into the depths of truth and understanding." Here is a piece that I wrote for this working:

In every soul, a story hides,
Beneath the surface, deep inside.
With open heart and eyes to see,
I'll seek the truth, judgment free.

8. Meditation: Spend some time in quiet meditation. Focus on your breath and the candle's flame. As you inhale and exhale, visualize yourself gaining insight and understanding, peering beneath the surface of things.

9. Journaling: Open your eyes and take your journal and pen. Write down any thoughts, images, or insights that came to you during the meditation or while gazing into the mirror.

10. Closing: Thank the elements, your guides, or any deities you work with for their guidance. Extinguish the candle.

11. Reflection: Take a moment to reflect on your experience. How did you feel during the ritual? What insights did you gain? How can you apply these insights to your life?

12. Repeat: You can repeat this ritual whenever you need guidance or wish to see beyond the surface in specific situations or if you want to see the true heart of a person.

CHAPTER TWELVE
WHEN THE WILD SOUL
SLEEPS

"When the magick sleeps, don't worry. It's the sun setting after a
long day, or the world taking a quiet breath in the still of the night.
It's not gone; it's just recharging. When it awakens, it will bring new
wonders, just like the morning sun or that first bloom of spring. So,
let it sleep, because the most powerful magick never disappears."

We have all been touched by death and the pain that comes with it. As
magick folk, we have come to learn that in spite of the hurt and the empty
space it leaves in our hearts, death is never truly an end but a time of movement, change, and transformation. Energy is energy is energy, and it never
ceases to exist. It simply takes on a new form and continues to create and
is a conduit for manifestation. I have walked hand in hand with death on
many occasions. I have helped to usher sweet, dear souls into the next leg
of their journey as an ordained minister, both in the Christian church and
as an independent minister.

I can honestly say that it has always been a peaceful part of my craft
and something that I don't take lightly. I have been there as many family
members have moved on and held hands with dear friends as they walked
those liminal spaces just before their final breath. It doesn't take away the
loss or the pain of not having them close, but it helps me to look at death
in a more holistic and profound way.

As the seasons swirl around us, we enter into the transition from light into darkness and back into light again. Life is a never-ending cycle. We move from the wild abandon of spring and summer into the time when nature's colors begin to transform, and then we march somberly into the season of winter and the stark, icy stillness and dormancy that overtakes the earth. Our lives seem to always be centered around transition. Those things that we wish we could control...we have no control over at all.

I became intimately acquainted with hope and renewal through visits from an unexpected stranger, the Green Wizard. I learned firsthand what a kind and gentle spirit can accomplish through him. I learned to listen more intently to what the earth teaches...all through him. I learned to trust the heart of faithful friends more. I learned to love someone who could do absolutely nothing for me other than be a friend and a magickal confidante...someone who represented purity of heart and selfless abandon.

It was just before Yule of 2015 that I learned that the Green Wizard had journeyed beyond the veil. He apparently collapsed on the sidewalk of a small town close to the Tennessee border. They took him to the hospital, where it was found that his heart was giving out. Boomer, his dog, was put in holding at the local animal shelter. He quietly slipped from this plane in his sleep. They found my name and Atlanta, Georgia, written on a sheet of paper in his pocket. The authorities assumed that I might be the next of kin. I explained that I was a friend and asked what happened to his dog. When I found out that he was at the local shelter, I remembered the promise that the Green Wizard had made to him...that he would never be alone. I called my cousin, who does animal rescue in North Carolina, and she arranged for someone who works with her to go and get Boomer and set up a fostering situation. There were so many more things that transpired due to his homelessness...especially since there was no identification of any kind associated with him and no direction as far as family or even a name...the one thing that was told to me by the person who made contact with me was that at least he knew friendship…there were many who passed on knowing nothing but rejection and hatred.

In my mind, though, I will always see him dancing on the wind. I can close my eyes and see his ruddy face, his eyes twinkling with hopes and dreams and always that sparkle of magick. He enjoyed the freedom of being who he was…an extension of the wild god. I can hear his hearty laugh echoing through the branches of the trees in the woods. He will forever be the embodiment of a nature spirit to me…always dancing with the moon, singing to the trees, and playing tag with the wind.

Am I sad? Yes…but I can never forget that wonderful spirit. He always looked for that bit of magick in all things…whether it be an old pair of sneakers…a dog considered a throw-away…or a weathered old wytch who seemed to be a little out of sorts himself.

I know, as change envelops each of our paths, that so many of us wait patiently for rebirth…in our own practice, journey, and even in our own spirit. It will be the same for my dear friend, the Green Wizard. He only sleeps now…we have known each other before in other lives and other magickal places. It is only a matter of time before we see each other again.

I am excited for him. Even in death, he would be privy to a new adventure….a fresh beginning coming that started with that December new moon. This was his chance to be reunited with his beloved Calliope…a chance to dance and finally fly among the stars. I am privileged to have been able to be a part of his magick.

His energy will always soar around me…sneaking up behind me when I least expect it…laughing heartily at the unexpected. He was a child of the moon and sun…the earth was his bed, and the grass was his pillow. He was friend to the winged and four-legged. He loved completely and wildly and unconditionally.

Another dear soul who made a lasting impact on my heart and life was the incomparable Cindy Maluna. We met through social media and became fast friends. She was a strong-spirited woman from the northeast who had fought her way through situations and circumstances that would cause most of us to fall apart. She was always willing to offer love, acceptance, and guidance, but she was also quick to call you out in a hot minute. I can remember one of the quotes she would use on me…sometimes quite regularly. Whenever I was feeling overwhelmed or feeling sorry for myself, (most of the time due to something I did). She would either text or call. I can still hear those words loud and clear, "For the love of the gods, be the wytch that you are…. or be the wytch you are called to be."

Talk about a wake-up call. It can be easy to lose ourselves in crisis or in the midst of troubles, especially when most of those come from situations we have created. Cindy was very much a sister and a mother at the same time…to all she came into contact with. She would call, and we would chat for long chunks of time…she would say that we spent that time solving the problems of the world, but in reality, we talked about magick and the seasons and the movement of the world around us and how we, as wytches could and would affect change.

Many years ago, I wrote a blog and just before Samhain, I had asked Cindy if she would write a piece for it. I share this as a tribute to her and to offer hope for those who may be struggling:

"Samhain. It means Summer's end. The end of a season…the end of the wytches year. The veil between the worlds is thin…the dead walk among the living…and many of us see and hear them. It's always been my favorite Sabbat… this year it took on a whole new meaning.

It's been a turbulent year for me….the end of a marriage, a new home…. the death* of a life I once knew. Deep in the woods…far from anyone….I feel the hedge wytches….they lived away from society….shunned for being different…feared or respected…they practiced their craft in solitude.

I've been shunned from my small town. Lies, accusations, misconceptions from friends and family…and like the Salem wytch trails….rumors spread like wildfire….fingers pointed…damage done. I've walked these woods each day… listening to the voices of the past….sometimes wailing like the banshees that cry in the howling wind...looking for answers....wondering if all I have lost is worth what I've gained.

Do we travel through our physical lives like the ghosts and spirits that slip through the veil? Do they regret their lives and the consequences of their actions? Do they haunt and pass through to feel...to touch once more what they had.... good or bad? When we die...I believe we have choices....to start fresh, or to come back with glimmers of the life we left...maybe it takes many lives lived to find the purpose...the soulmate...the connection that will send us to the divine afterlife....the completeness. Could we possibly be just lost souls traveling through the veil looking for that connection? Seeking...searching.

I've found many answers in this dead season....and I'll find more in coming dark months....it's always been my time. As many tears as I've cried for what is past....I also see a glimmer of light....the glint of a sword...the flick of a cape....the brush of The Morrigan...and I've found a connection of magick with a dear friend....a goal to build a sanctuary of magick and Nature...a haven for the ancient hedge wytches that pass through the deep woods that surround us...our voices will carry on the traditions...the love of the land....a time lost in the Mists. In the dark, cold ashes of the Samhain fires new growth will be rise....new lives will be lived....and magick will carry on."

I have learned many things over the course of my journey as a wytch. Most of what I have learned is to get over myself and to do the work required. I have walked through my own share of tribulations and felt my share of hurts and pain, but I have tried with everything I have to always be teachable and willing to glean knowledge and magick from any and every situation and every stumble. I have learned one thing for certain in all my years...with magick, nothing ever completely dies.

Exercise: "Awakening Your Inner Magick"

Objective: This exercise aims to help you tap into and nurture the inner magick that resides within you, fostering a sense of wonder and empowerment in your everyday life.

Instructions:

1. Quiet Space:

Find a quiet and comfortable space where you won't be disturbed. This could be indoors or outdoors, depending on your preference.

2. Journal or Notebook:

Have a journal or notebook and a pen ready to record your thoughts, experiences, and insights.

3. Setting Intentions:

Start by setting your intention for this exercise: to awaken and embrace the innate magick within you, allowing it to manifest in your daily life.

4. Inner Reflection:

Close your eyes and take a few deep breaths to center yourself. Imagine that you're descending into the depths of your inner self, where your magick resides.

5. Childhood Wonder:

Recall a moment from your childhood when you felt a sense of wonder and enchantment. It could be a memory of seeing a rainbow, blowing dandelion seeds, or discovering a hidden place in nature.

6. Embrace Your Inner Child:

Reconnect with your inner child and that feeling of unbridled curiosity and belief in the extraordinary. Imagine your inner child standing before you, ready to guide you on this magickal journey.

7. Visualization:

Visualize a radiant, glowing ball of light within your chest. This ball represents your inner magick, a source of limitless potential.

8. Connection with Nature:

Imagine stepping into a lush forest or a tranquil natural setting. Feel the energy of the earth beneath your feet and the rustling of leaves in the breeze.

9. Elemental Connection:

Connect with the four elements:

Earth: Feel the stability and grounding energy of the earth.

Air: Sense the gentle caress of the wind on your skin.

Fire: Visualize the warm, glowing light of a candle or campfire.

Water: Imagine the soothing flow of a stream or the gentle lap of waves.

10. Magickal Affirmations:

Repeat magickal affirmations to yourself, such as:

"I am a conduit of magickal energy."

"I embrace the wonder and mystery of the world."

"My inner magick flows freely within me."

11. Journal Reflection:

Open your eyes and return to your physical surroundings. Write in your journal about the sensations and emotions you experienced during this inner magick exploration.

12. Everyday Magick:

Throughout your day, be mindful of moments that feel magickal or extraordinary. It could be a beautiful sunrise, a serendipitous encounter, or a sudden burst of inspiration.

13. Creative Expression:

Engage in a creative activity that allows your inner magick to flow. This could be writing, drawing, painting, crafting, or any form of artistic expression that resonates with you.

14. Gratitude:

Express gratitude for the magick within and around you. Recognize that you are a conduit for the extraordinary, and it can manifest in your daily life.

15. Regular Practice:

Commit to regularly practicing this exercise and nurturing your inner magick. Embrace the belief that your life can be a magickal journey filled with wonder and possibility.

Let's Do the Working:

Ritual: Awakening the Magick Inside

Items Needed:
- A quiet, sacred space where you won't be disturbed.
- A red or orange candle (for passion and energy).
- A lighter or matches.
- A small, heatproof bowl or cauldron.
- A piece of paper and a pen.
- Your favorite incense (for purification and focus).
- A journal and a pen.

Steps:

1. Preparation: Find a quiet and comfortable space where you can sit or stand. Clear the space of any distractions and clutter.

2. Cleansing (optional): Light your favorite incense and let the smoke waft around you and through the ritual space. As you do this, visualize any stagnant energy dissipating, leaving you purified and focused.

3. Light the Candle: Light the red or orange candle and place it in front of you. As you do this, set your intention for the ritual: to rekindle the fire and passion of magick within yourself, to invigorate your practice.

4. Meditation: Close your eyes and take a few deep breaths. Visualize

a glowing ember within your core, representing your magickal energy. See this ember slowly growing into a roaring flame, filling you with passion and energy for your magickal journey.

5. Affirmation: While focusing on the candle's flame, repeat an affirmation, such as,

Awaken, awaken, the magick within,
Ignite like a fire, let it begin.
In my heart, in my soul, it's been waiting so long,
To dance with the stars, to sing its own song.
With each breath that I take, with each beat of my heart,
Feel the enchantment, let the sorcery start.
In the whispers of leaves, in the moon's gentle glow,
The magick's alive, let your true self show.
Embrace the unknown, let your spirit take flight,
In the realm of the mystic, where day turns to night.
Awaken, dear wytch, as my power runs free,
The magick is waiting, it's all within me.

6. Write Your Intentions: Take a piece of paper and a pen. Write down your magickal intentions and goals, no matter how big or small they may be. This is a declaration of your renewed commitment to your magickal path.

7. Burn the Paper: Carefully hold the paper over the candle's flame and let it burn. As it turns to ash, visualize your intentions manifesting, and feel the fire and passion growing within you.

8. Journaling: Open your eyes and take your journal and pen. Write down your thoughts and feelings, any insights or inspirations that came to you during the ritual.

9. Closing: Thank the elements, your guides, or any deities you work with for their guidance. Extinguish the candle.

10. Reflection: Take a moment to reflect on your experience. How did you feel during the ritual? How can you nurture the renewed fire and passion in your magickal practice moving forward?

11. Repeat: You can repeat this ritual whenever you feel the need to rekindle the passion and energy in your magickal journey.

CHAPTER THIRTEEN
REIGNITING THE FLAMES
OF MAGICK

"Let the flames of passion ignite your magick, for it is the fuel that kindles the sparks of intention and propels them into manifestation. Embrace your deepest passions and infuse them into your craft, for in their fiery embrace, your magick shall truly flourish."

Passion is a word that has become overused in this day and age. It has moved into the same position as the word love. It has been used for anything from ice cream to an insatiable feeling of eroticism. I want to take you on a journey using the definition outlined above to understand Passion when associated with our magickal path or our spiritual practices.

In many religions, there is a moment of epiphany or a 'salvation' moment. Even the magickal path is not one exempt from this. We have all had those 'aha' moments within our practices and these are the moments from which our growth is normally spring-boarded.

In the realm of magick, there often comes a time when the fire that once burned brightly within us begins to wane. It's not uncommon for practitioners to experience periods of stagnation or doubt, where the once-vibrant connection to the mystical arts feels distant. However, don't be afraid, for in this chapter, we will explore ways to rekindle the passion in your magick, reigniting that powerful flame that lies within you. It's crucial to recognize that the journey of a magickal practitioner is not a constant upward spiral.

Much like the tides of the ocean, our connection to magick has its ebbs and flows. Accepting this natural rhythm is the first step toward renewing your enthusiasm.

Take a moment to think about why you fell in love with magick to begin with. Was it to heal or offer healing, to explore the mysteries of the universe, or was it to manifest your desires? Reconnecting with your original purpose can reignite your passion. I have created a section in my grimoire with this information and also a mini collage that represents my magickal passions. When I feel less than magickal, I turn to that section of my book and am once again transported back to the moment when I first fell in love with the Craft.

I can remember the first time I truly felt the power of magick. I was only a child. I was raised on a farm in North Carolina, and I spent most of my days wandering dirt paths and napping on forest floors. When I close my eyes, I am transported back to those same feelings and emotions that moved through me even then. I can smell the pine and cedar and hear the wind singing in my ears. Take a moment….let your mind go back to that first time that magick found you. Where were you? What were you doing? Do you remember sights, scents?

When was the last time that you escaped the mundane and delved into the world of magick? As witches, it is easy for us to say that this is a frame of mind. It may be, but even we can get stuck in a rut. "Sending healing!" "Lighting a candle for you!" The practice becomes almost mechanical for the most basic things. Don't get me wrong, not everything needs to be a full-on ritual, but magick must still pull from that most intimate part of us. It must flow from our strongest and deepest intentions. Lighting the candle is only a piece of the process. Without our emotions, intentions, and, yes, even passion, it is only a lit candle. When I go into the woods, I go with the intent that it will be an experience steeped in magick and power. Most of that time is spent sitting…quietly listening to what the world and the spirits around me have to say.

Magick is a vast and ever-evolving field. Sometimes, a lack of passion can be a result of feeling stagnant in your knowledge. Dive into learning by picking up new books, attending workshops, or exploring different traditions and practices. This thirst for knowledge can spark renewed enthusiasm. I read all the time. I don't just read books exclusive to my own belief system. I delve into areas that may be out of my scope of knowledge or other types of magick just so that I know more about the practices of others. I have friends from all magickal walks of life and I respect and honor their paths as much as I do my own.

Nature is a wellspring of magickal energy. Spend time in natural surroundings, whether it's a forest, a beach, or a park. By now, you realize my love for nature and the woods. Nature itself, is a huge instigator of magick for me. Anytime I visit or spend time with nature and its creatures, magick abounds. It has always been like going home for me, and it always finds a way to add more spark and excitement to my journey. It is in nature that my magick seems the strongest. It is in partnering with the elements and the spirits of nature that my spirit is strengthened and my passion for magick rekindled.

Rituals can be another part of the heartbeat of magick. I revisit your daily, weekly, or seasonal rituals on a regular basis and am constantly creating new ones. The act of performing rituals can reignite your passion by grounding you in the present moment and allowing you to channel your intent with focused energy. As you will see in this book, most of my rituals aren't hard or overly difficult. I use different objects to represent whatever is needed in my workings and I have found that my own words hold more power for me than spells that I glean from others. When I first began practicing wytchcraft, I was nervous about writing my own spells, rituals, and rhymes, but as I have practiced and realized that magick flows from what is inside, it has become a part of me and an integral part of my magickal workings.

Journaling is a powerful tool for self-discovery. I talk about journaling quite a bit in my 'Let's Do the Workings' sections. I keep a magickal journal, completely separate from my grimoire or my book of shadows, where I record experiences, thoughts, and dreams related to my own magickal life. This self-reflection has helped me to identify patterns, obstacles, and areas where I have grown or need to grow. I have found that keeping my journal by my bed at night allows me to record dreams when they are fresh in my mind and to sometimes see the symbolism that they hold more quickly.

Community is a large part of keeping the passion within your practice. I am a solitary wytch, but I have found that by having friends and colleagues throughout the many types and teachings of magick are crucial. I don't want to become one of those stoic, angry wytches who are so afraid of anything outside the scope of my understanding to keep me stagnant in my own path. Questions and curiosity are integral to moving forward in magick, and it keeps us from locking ourselves away in our own little box. It helps us to be able to look at the world of magick and witchcraft holistically and with a broader understanding of what magick is capable of.

Don't be afraid to experiment with your magickal practice. Always be willing to try new things and push the boundaries of what you believe is possible. Innovation and creativity can reignite the spark of passion by challenging you to see magick in new ways. Again, I am not going to be someone who tells another wytch that what they are doing is wrong. I am the one who will be right in the middle of the workings, looking over shoulders with a sense of wonder as to what they are creating. Allow that sense of wonder in you to always look for new things to try. I look at this approach akin to the way a child looks at things. My nephews are in awe of everything at their ages now. They ask questions, they allow themselves to be enamored with the ordinary so that they are able to see more when the extraordinary happens. I have watched far too many wytches fall into the same trap as the Christian church…they get so caught up in the ritual or the working and actually forget to look for the magick.   No matter how old I get, I will always look for the magick first. Everything else will fall into place.

Challenges and obstacles are not signs of failure but opportunities for growth. Embrace them with an open heart. Overcoming difficulties in your magickal journey can reignite your passion as you discover your inner strength. I can't even begin to tell you how many times I have had to re-do a spell because I did something wrong or my intent wasn't on point, or I just wasn't feeling it at the moment. None of these things mean that you failed. The magickal journey is like any other journey. There will be detours, unplanned situations, and even tumbles as you walk it out. The key, for me, has been to get up, brush myself off, and start all over again. The only failure I have ever experienced is when I didn't try.

If you find yourself stuck in a rut, seek guidance from a trusted mentor or spiritual advisor. Their wisdom and perspective can provide insights that help you navigate your magickal path with renewed passion and purpose. As I wrote earlier, Cindy Maluna was one person who heard all about my failures, successes, and tests. She was quick to offer support but wouldn't allow me to sit and lick my wounds either. It is important to have people that we trust who can speak into our lives with truth and authority without us getting our feelings hurt and tucking our tails between our legs and not trying again. Cindy loved to tell me that I was stronger than any circumstance that came knocking. In return, I try to offer that same type of support and assistance to those who have come into my life and have asked me to take on the role of mentor and friend. Truth is imperative, but it is also important that that truth be tempered with genuine caring and the desire to see someone else win.

Each morning, when I wake up, I stand to my feet, audibly greet the new day, and then offer up a prayer to make that passion for magick come alive in me. I ask to be vigilant, and I ask for help to make a concerted effort to see the magick around me. I make it a point to stand in the window of the bedroom or outside with my face to the sun. I speak to my own heart, letting it know that magick is always afoot and that it is up to me to be watchful. Here is the prayer that I offer each morning:

"May the magick within me awaken and dance with every step I take today, in every moment that unfolds before me. May I look for the extraordinary in the ordinary and may my passion for magick be a guiding light, illuminating the wonder that exists around me. May I see that magick… that spark in all things today."

Rekindling the passion in your magick is a journey into self more than anything and is a conduit for growth. It requires patience, self-compassion, and a willingness to explore new horizons. It is, in reality, a relationship, and relationships must be nurtured and kept fresh, and the work must be put into them. Remember that the flame of magick within you is always there, waiting to be reignited. With dedication and a sense of wonder, you can fan the flames and continue your mystical journey with renewed zeal and vitality.

What made you fall in love with magick? What made you want to pursue the path that you are walking? What is it that makes your heart soar when you think about your own relationship with the magick and world around you?

What Is My Passion? My passion is to live a Magickal life. My passion is to live a life guided by the Sun and the Moon and the Earth and the Wind and Water and Fire. My passion is to hold close the teachings of those who have come and gone before me. My passion is to be sun-kissed, wind-burned, drenched and dirty. My passion is to be covered in hugs and kisses by the humans I love. My passion is to look down at my shirt and laugh in wonder as to whose hair I just found stuck to me (is it a cat whisker? or dog fur?). I refuse to worry myself sick over what is right and wrong about what I practice. I still have something that is more than valuable: *Instinct.* The ancients didn't have star charts and iPhones that told them that the moon was full. They knew.

My passion is to know myself better than anyone else knows me and to embrace every moment of life around me. It is not always going to be wonderful and beautiful...but it will always be what I choose to make of it. And, finally, Where is my place? Wherever I am. My place is home....no matter where I may be.

Exercise: "Discovering Your Magickal Passion"

Objective: This exercise encourages you to explore and uncover your specific areas of passion and interest within the realm of magick, guiding you toward a more fulfilling magickal practice.

Instructions:

1. Serene Space:

Find a quiet and serene space where you can concentrate without distractions.

2. Journal or Notebook:

Have a journal or notebook and a pen ready to record your thoughts, discoveries, and insights.

3. Setting Intentions:

Begin by setting your intention for this exercise: to explore and identify the aspects of magick that truly resonate with you and ignite your passion.

4. Magickal Reflection:

Close your eyes and take a few deep breaths to center yourself. Visualize a serene, magickal space within your mind where you can explore your magickal passions.

5. Past Experiences:

Reflect on any past experiences with magick or the occult. These could include rituals, spells, divination, or any magickal practices you've tried.

6. Curiosities and Interests:

List the aspects of magick or the occult that have always intrigued you or sparked your curiosity. These might be specific traditions, symbols, tools, or practices.

7. Personal Values:

Consider your personal values and beliefs. What aspects of magick align with your spiritual or ethical principles? Write down any values that are important to you.

8. Memorable Moments:

Recall any magickal experiences or moments when you felt deeply connected to the magickal world. What were you doing, and how did it make you feel?

9. Role Models:

Think about magickal practitioners, authors, or mentors who inspire you. What aspects of their practice or teachings resonate with you?

10. Current Exploration:

If you're currently exploring magick, take note of the practices or topics that excite you the most. What do you look forward to studying or practicing?

11. Core Passions:

Analyze your reflections and identify the core passions and interests that stand out. These are the aspects of magick that truly resonate with you.

12. Dedicate Time:

Dedicate time to explore and deepen your understanding of your chosen magickal passions. This could involve reading books, studying, attending workshops, or practicing rituals.

13. Journal Your Journey:

Regularly update your journal with your experiences, insights, and discoveries as you delve deeper into your chosen magickal passions. Document your progress and any challenges you encounter.

14. Connect with Others:

Connect with magickal communities, forums, or groups that focus on your chosen passions. Engaging with like-minded individuals can provide valuable support and inspiration.

15. Gratitude:

Express gratitude for the path of magick you're exploring and the fulfillment it brings to your spiritual journey. Recognize that your passion in magick is a personal and evolving journey.

Let's Do the Working:

Ritual: Reigniting the Flames of Magick

Intention: This ritual is designed to help you reconnect with your inner magickal energy, rekindle your sense of wonder, and reignite your passion for the mystical arts.

Items Needed:
- A quiet and private space where you won't be disturbed
- A white candle (representing purity and clarity)
- A journal or notebook
- A pen or pencil
- A small dish with sand or salt
- A fireproof container or cauldron
- A lighter or matches
- Any magickal tools or symbols that are personally significant to you (optional)

Procedure:
1. Cleansing and Grounding:

Stand in the center of your chosen space and take several deep breaths. Visualize any negative or stagnant energy leaving your body and sinking into the earth.

2. Setting Intentions:

Light the white candle and say a simple prayer or affirmation to set your intentions. Express your desire to reignite your magickal flame and reconnect with your inner power.

3. Creating Sacred Space:

If you have any magickal tools or symbols that are personally meaningful, arrange them in your ritual space. This could include crystals, tarot cards, or symbols of the elements.

4. The Flame of Purification:

Light the white candle and let its flame symbolize the purity of your intentions. Gaze into the flame, focusing on its clarity and energy. Feel the warmth and illumination it provides.

5. Journal Reflection:

Open your journal or notebook and write down any thoughts or feelings that come to mind about your connection to magick and the mystical. Reflect on why you were drawn to these practices in the first place.

6. Sacred Flame Visualization:

Close your eyes and visualize a small, magickal flame at the center of your being. Imagine this flame growing and expanding with each breath, filling your entire body with magickal energy. Feel its warmth and power.

7. Words of Empowerment:

Speak aloud words of empowerment and affirmation. For example: "I am a vessel of magick. My inner flame burns bright, and I am filled with the power of the mystic."

8. Symbolic Release:

Take the piece of paper and write down any doubts, fears, or blocks that have hindered your connection to magick. Place the paper into the fireproof container.

9. Igniting the Fire:

Light the paper on fire using the candle's flame. As it burns, visualize your doubts and fears transforming into ashes and being released.

10. The Elemental Dance:

Stand and hold your arms open wide. Imagine yourself dancing with the elements—earth, air, fire, and water. Feel their energy flowing through you, reinvigorating your magickal spirit.

11. Gratitude and Closing:

Express gratitude to the elements, the candle's flame, and the magickal energy you've invoked. Thank them for reigniting the flames of your magick.

12. Journal Reflection (Part 2):

Write in your journal again, recording your experiences during the ritual. Note any insights, inspirations, or intentions for your renewed magickal practice.

13. Closing the Ritual:

Snuff out the candle and take a few moments to sit quietly in the dark. Know that the flame within you burns brightly, and your connection to magick has been rekindled.

This ritual is a personal and powerful way to reignite your passion for magick and reconnect with your inner mystic. As you continue your journey, may the flames of your magickal spirit burn ever brighter.

CHAPTER FOURTEEN
THE ROAD BACK HOME

"Returning to the roots of your path is like coming back home to old friends. It's about rekindling the connection to the natural world around us, finding comfort in the moon's glow, and rediscovering the power within yourself that you may have forgotten was there or overlooked. Just as the road back home brings comfort and familiarity, so does the journey back to your path. It's a reminder that magick is not something outside of us; it's a part of who we are, waiting to be embraced and understood."

It has been many many decades since I last lived among my kin and some of the places that only exist in my memories now. That old house of Maw-Maw's in Fairfield has been gone for years. Even the newer place downhill from the cemetery is now someone else's home. The old homeplaces will never be the same since the aunts and uncles and all the grandparents have gone. I drive by them when I visit Ma and Pop and the houses stand quiet and abandoned. In my mind's eye, I can still hear the screams of laughter and the stories that danced around the rooms. I can hear MawMaw strumming on her old guitar, singing "Set Your Fields On Fire" with my aunt Audrey harmonizing in the background.

It seems like only yesterday, I was a young'un sitting on the porch with a basket of beans or peas sitting between my legs and adding to the bucket of peas MawMaw had already shelled before us grandkids got there. There were always tales to be told and the problems of the world to be solved over a basket of unshelled peas.

There never was a time that I didn't believe that magick was real. It was a part of our day to day life, no matter how far from home we managed to travel. We were always taught to look for the unusual or the impossible and to offer it a chance to live and move amongst us. It seems that the things we were taught to be afraid of weren't fear-worthy at all and the things we weren't scared of were the things that most folks ran from.

There is a quote from a 1940 Thomas Wolfe novel, that states, "You can never go home again." This saying is meant to show us that nostalgia can cause us to see the past through filtered glasses. We tend to look back and see only the good and remember those in our past as stronger, better, and far more magickal. I agree with this quote for the most part. Many of the places and people who have held a strong influence in my life and my practices are nothing more than places on maps and memories now.

You may not be able to go home again, but you can take home with you wherever you go. I have found that in my most trying times, the memories of MawMaw, Nannie, and all the aunts and uncles sustain me. It is in looking back at their strengths and trials that my own strength and power are shown the strongest. I have found that no matter the location, I am home when I am in the woods.

Home is not a place; it's a feeling that lives deep within your heart and soul. It's the warmth of familiar smiles, the comfort of shared laughter, and the hugs of those you love. Home is where you find comfort and acceptance and can truly be yourself without fear or judgment.

It's not defined by the walls that surround you but by the memories etched into your very soul. Home is the aroma of a favorite meal cooking in the kitchen, the softness of your childhood blanket, and the echo of laughter from years gone by.

Home is a haven of love and a sanctuary from the storms of life. It's where you find refuge in the arms of those who care for you, a place where you can rest your tired and weary heart and find strength for the challenges ahead.

Home is not a place on a map; it's a place in your heart where the people you love reside and where you, in turn, are cherished. It's a feeling that transcends physical boundaries and remains with you, no matter where life's journey may take you."

I know that in today's world, we are bombarded with the stresses of work, family, and survival in general. We, as wytches, aren't as isolated as our predecessors. They were afforded, either by necessity or by fear of the local townsfolk, the ability to live within those liminal spaces away from the prying or judgmental eyes of society.

In a day when social media and technology eliminates the luxury of anonymity and creates limits to the amount of ferality we are allowed to attain, we still have options.   I have allowed the wildness of the world around me to inhabit me. I am no less or more than those parts of my magick that I allow to transcend the boundaries assigned by mankind.

As we move through daily responsibilities and do our 'mundane' jobs, we forget that it is more than fine to be different. Conformity has become a place of comfort for most of us in our path to magick. I have found that I am far more comfortable taking off the mask of expectation that human-kind has put on me and walking or running in authenticity.

Over my life, I have been called many things.   Most of those I refuse to own or answer to. I have been called a hick, a hillbilly, a fag, and a devil worshipper. I may or may not be all of those, but I choose which names I answer to and which ones are a true representation of who I am.

I remember the first time someone called me a hick. I was flabbergast-ed. I couldn't believe that someone would see the rich culture of magick and history in my family and use a word that made us sound uneducated, basic, and unsavory. It was in that moment that I decided that I would take ownership of the word and use it to my benefit.

The word 'hick' has always been connected to people from the country who are considered to be stupid or have very little life experience. Such a contradiction, to be honest, of all the country folk I have known in my life. As I researched my family and dug into the essence of who each person was, I found no stupidity at all and a multitude of life experiences that made each one a complex and naturally magickal being.

Country folk have a certain attitude that was born out of necessity and survival instincts. We are folks who, if told we can't or shouldn't do something, will go out of our way to show you that it can be done, if nothing else, just to spite you. We are of strong constitution and have survived centuries of judgment and ridicule.

No matter how far from home I am, I will always carry the fortitude that my kin have passed down. I don't care what others think of me. I am stronger than that. I live a life steeped in magick, humor, and tales of where I came from and who I came from.

Several weeks ago, I went back to visit my family. I made it my purpose to revisit some of the old places that I remembered from my childhood. It seemed strange to drive up weed covered gravel roads that once wound up to old homesteads and see that the only thing left was a chimney. It was as if I could hear the laughter, singing, and old stories moving around that old smokestack. It made me think that energy doesn't disappear…it only changes, shifts.

That is the reason that those who have passed beyond the veil don't seem so distant to me. Each one is still so much a part of my spirit…my makeup…my magick. For so many years, I saw myself as broken and not worthy of my own heritage. I looked back and saw strength and passion and independence that I only dreamed of. It never occurred to me that they were a part of me the whole time. These characteristics were in my DNA before I was ever even a gleam in Ma and Pop's eyes.

It took me being able to look for and see them in myself. They were there, but I was overlooking them and keeping them hidden for far too long. As I get older, I definitely see Thula's independence, MawMaw's strength and passion, and even Zeb's second sight.

I have learned that these are qualities to be embraced, not to be hidden or to run from. Passions shift as we move into the crone or sage years. I have found that my passion has moved from concentrating on my own success and happiness to helping others to find their passion…to help them see their own brightness and to walk in the magick that flows through them. I look at the wytches of the past. Most offered service to the community around them. They looked for ways to help the common man when government and lifestyles weren't conducive to the success of the people.

I have conjured a life for myself where magick is the guiding force. I am definitely a part of this world but choose to also live a life separated from it, to a degree. As I have discussed, I am most at home in the woods, surrounded by moss and trees and wildlife. These were all gifts given to me by the family who came before. I am so much of a culmination of the best parts of my kinfolk.

As I write this, I feel the energy of those who paved the way for me. I am encircled by the love of centuries of Gaddys, Piggs, Hildreths, Medlins, and Trulls. There are so many more surnames that join that symphony of hearts and I was birthed as a tribute and testament to those hearts and spirits.

A few years ago, I wrote a poem that describes that feeling of home, no matter how far away I may venture:

Take Home With You"
In a world of constant motion, never still,
Where paths diverge, and fates fulfill,
Remember this, my dear, my muse,
You carry home, you cannot lose.
Take home with you, wherever you roam,
In your heart, it finds its own sweet home.
It's not a place, four walls, or door,
But a feeling, an essence, forevermore.

In the twinkle of starlight, or the sun's embrace,
In a distant land or your birthplace,
Home is the love that warms your soul,
A comfort, a refuge, making you whole.
Through deserts vast or oceans blue,
In every sky's ever-changing hue,
You're never alone, never apart,
For home resides within your heart.
So when the world feels cold and gray,
And you yearn for home, so far away,
Just close your eyes, let your spirit be free,
Take home with you, wherever you may be.

Magick and witchcraft are very much a part of that home-like feeling to me. They provide a sense of returning to a place of comfort, familiarity, and a connection to something greater in my own personal practice. Just as returning home after a long vacation, or visiting the places you grew up in can bring a feeling of security and belonging, the practice of magick offers a similar sense of being in touch with a deeper, aspect of myself and the universe.

I find that when I am at my most frustrated or my most annoyed, that just a moment to remind myself of the magick around me fulfills that need for peace and calm and understanding. Magick and Wytchcraft help me to take a step back and look at a situation through those eyes instead of the eyes of a frantic, stressed out, reactive human. I find comfort in the unorthodox ways that magick has shown me how to deal with anger, sadness, fear, and even ecstatic joy. I have learned, as I look through the lens of magick, that the world around me is far more temporal than I had thought. Nothing lasts forever, and I have control of how things affect me and how I respond. Magick is a powerful tool when it comes to manipulating the energy around me.

Is everything in my life perfect? Far from it. I have found, though, that with the right attitude and connection to my ancestors and to the magick folk in my circle of friends, I can call on them when I feel less than my magickal self. It is important to remember as we walk our own magickal paths…Magick doesn't have to be hard. It doesn't have to be perfect. It is a deeply personal and intuitive journey, where intentions and the authenticity of your practice hold more power than any ritual or spell. Embrace your unique path and trust that magick that flows through you.

It is important to remember who we are:

"We are quicksilver, a fleeting shadow, a distant sound…our home has no boundaries beyond which we cannot pass. We live in music, in a flash of color…we live on the wind and in the sparkle of a star." —Endora, Bewitched, Season 1: "Be it Ever So Mortgaged"

As a Wytch, Wherever we are is home.

Exercise: "Mapping Your Inner Home"

Objective: To discover and strengthen your connection to your inner home, a place of emotional and spiritual refuge.

Instructions:

1. Find a Quiet Space: Begin by selecting a quiet and comfortable space where you won't be disturbed. Sit or lie down in a relaxed position.

2. Close Your Eyes: Close your eyes and take a few deep breaths to center yourself. Inhale deeply through your nose and exhale slowly through your mouth. With each exhale, release any tension or stress you may be carrying.

3. Visualize Your Inner Home: Imagine a place within yourself where you always feel safe, loved, and at peace. This can be a physical location, a feeling, or even a combination of both. It could be a childhood home, a

favorite vacation spot, or simply a space where you feel completely accepted and cherished.

4. Explore Your Inner Home: Once you've identified your inner home, explore it in your mind. Notice the details—colors, textures, scents, and sounds. What makes this place special to you? How does it make you feel?

5. Embrace Your Emotions: As you explore your inner home, pay attention to your emotions. Are you feeling a sense of comfort, warmth, or contentment? Let those feelings wash over you.

6. Journal Your Experience: After your visualization, take out a journal or a piece of paper. Write down your experience, describing your inner home in detail. What did you see, hear, and feel? How did it make you feel emotionally and spiritually?

7. Create an Inner Home Affirmation: Based on your experience, craft a simple affirmation that connects you to your inner home. For example, "I carry my inner home with me wherever I go, and I am always safe and loved."

8. Daily Reflection: Make it a practice to reflect on your inner home and recite your affirmation daily. This will help you carry this sense of home with you wherever you are, providing emotional support and comfort during challenging times.

9. Extend Your Inner Home: As you become more connected to your inner home, consider how you can extend this sense of home to the physical spaces in your life. How can you make your surroundings reflect the warmth and comfort you've discovered within?

10. Share Your Experience: If you're comfortable, share your experience with a trusted friend or journal about it regularly. This can deepen your connection to your inner home and create a sense of community around the concept of finding home within.

Let's Do the Working:

I like to call this ritual, "Southern Comfort: Rooted in Home"

Objective: To infuse the essence of Southern hospitality and comfort into your sense of home, no matter where you are.

Participants: This ritual is designed for solitary practitioners but can be adapted for group settings.

Materials Needed:
    – A small piece of red fabric or a red cloth bag.
    – A handful of soil or earth from a place that feels like home to you in the South.
    – A small piece of cedar or pine bark.
    – A small white candle.
    – A quiet and comfortable space.

Ritual Steps:
    1. Setting the Space:
        Find a quiet and comfortable space where you can sit or stand comfortably.
        Place the red fabric, the soil, the piece of cedar or pine bark, and the white candle within your reach.
    2. Centering Yourself:
        Take a few deep breaths to center yourself in the present moment. Inhale deeply through your nose and exhale slowly through your mouth.
        Close your eyes and visualize a scene that embodies the essence of home for you. It could be a front porch, a welcoming kitchen, or a cozy living room.
    3. Preparing the Red Fabric:
        Hold the red fabric in your hands and infuse it with your intention for creating a "home mentality."

Visualize the fabric as a symbol of warmth, comfort, and hospitality.

4. Gathering Earth Energy:

Take a handful of soil or earth from the place that feels like home to you.

Hold it in your hands and feel the connection to that place. Imagine the energy of that land flowing into you.

5. Cedar or Pine Blessing:

Hold the piece of cedar or pine bark in your hands, recognizing it as a symbol of Southern trees and forests.

Visualize the strength, resilience, and shelter they provide.

6. Creating the Pouch:

Place the soil and the piece of cedar or pine bark inside the red fabric or cloth bag.

Tie the bag closed, sealing the energy within.

7. Candle Illumination:

Light the white candle, symbolizing purity and illumination.

Hold the lit candle over the sealed fabric bag, allowing the wax to drip and form a seal over the knot.

As you do, say aloud or in your mind: "By the light of this candle, I seal the essence of the comforts of home within this bag. Wherever I go, home goes with me."

8. Daily Practice:

Keep the sealed fabric bag with you, perhaps in your bag or pocket.

Whenever you need to reconnect with your "home mentality," hold the bag in your hands, close your eyes, and visualize the warm, welcoming energy it contains.

NOTIONS, POTIONS, AND RECIPES

Horned God Incense

Ingredients:

1. Patchouli: Patchouli represents the earthy and grounding qualities often associated with the Horned God.

2. Cedarwood: Cedarwood adds a deep and woody note, symbolizing the strength of the wild.

3. Juniper Berries: Juniper berries are connected to the wild and the untamed, making them a fitting addition.

4. Frankincense Resin: Frankincense adds a touch of spirituality and reverence to your blend.

5. Myrrh Resin: Myrrh is protective and grounding, often used in rituals connected to the Horned God.

6. Oakmoss: Oakmoss is reminiscent of the forest floor, bringing the energy of the wilderness to your incense.

7. Black Pepper: Black pepper adds a spicy and energetic note, representing the fiery aspect of the Horned God.

Goddess Incense

Ingredients:

1. Rose Petals: Dried rose petals represent love, beauty, and the nurturing qualities often associated with the goddess.

2. Lavender: Lavender brings a sense of peace, grace, and tranquility to your Goddess incense.

3. Jasmine Flowers: Jasmine is known for its sensuality and connection to the goddess, making it a wonderful addition.

4. Frankincense Resin: Frankincense adds a touch of spirituality and mysticism to your blend.

5. Myrrh Resin: Myrrh is grounding and protective, often used in goddess rituals.

6. Sandalwood: Sandalwood provides a woody and grounding base note for your incense.

7. Moonstone Powder (Optional): Moonstone is associated with the moon, femininity, and intuition.

Ancestors Incense

Ingredients:

1. Graveyard Pine or Yew (Pinch): Gather a small pinch of graveyard pine or yew needles from a sacred space where you feel a connection to spirits.

2. Cedar (½ Part): Cedarwood is grounding and protective, making it a suitable choice for ancestor work.

3. Mistletoe (Pinch): Mistletoe is associated with healing and protection, making it a valuable addition.

4. Sandalwood (1 Part): Sandalwood provides a woody and grounding base note to your incense.

5. Orange Peel (½ Part): Dried orange peel adds a bright and uplifting citrus note to the blend.

6. Copal (1 Part): Copal resin is traditionally used in spiritual and ancestral rituals for its sweet and purifying qualities.

7. Lavender (½ Part): Lavender adds a touch of calm and peace to your

incense.

8. Tobacco (1 Part): Tobacco is a sacred plant in many indigenous traditions and can be used to facilitate communication with ancestors.

9. Whiskey Essential Oil: A few drops of whiskey essential oil will provide a unique and symbolic touch to your blend.

Forest Incense

Ingredients:

1. Pine Needles: Fresh or dried pine needles are the cornerstone of a forest-scented incense, providing that unmistakable woodland aroma.

2. Cedarwood Shavings or Chips: Cedarwood adds depth and a rich earthy scent to your forest incense.

3. Juniper Berries: Juniper berries contribute a refreshing and slightly resinous fragrance, reminiscent of forest air.

4. Oakmoss: Oakmoss is a fragrant lichen found on trees in forests. It has a woody, earthy scent with a touch of greenness.

5. Frankincense Resin: Frankincense adds a mystical and grounding element to the forest blend.

6. Balsam Fir Needles: offer the scent of the woodlands and a soothing, calming feeling

Go On, Git Powder (For Banishing)

Ingredients:

1. Red Brick Dust: Red brick dust is a traditional Southern hoodoo ingredient known for its protective and barrier properties. It's often used to keep negativity at bay.

2. Cayenne Pepper: Cayenne pepper adds fiery energy to the mixture,

making it effective for driving away obstacles and unwanted people or situations.

3. Rattlesnake Shed Skin: Represents transformation, renewal, and protection. It's believed to ward off negative energies and help initiate personal growth.

4. Mullein Leaf: Mullein is associated with protection and courage. It can help dispel fear and unwanted influences.

5. Magnetite or Lodestone Dust: Magnetite or lodestone is known for its magnetic properties. It can be used to draw in positive energy while repelling negativity.

Heart of the South Incense

Ingredients:

1. Snake Shed Skin: Represents transformation, shedding old habits, and renewal. It can be used to facilitate personal growth and change.

2. Fire Ant Nest Dirt: Fire ants are known for their fierce protection. Fire ant chitin can be used to create a protective barrier or ward against negative influences.

3. Spanish Moss: Spanish moss is a mystical plant associated with hidden knowledge and dreams. It can enhance psychic abilities and divination.

4. Wild Mint: Wild mint is known for its refreshing and invigorating scent. It can be used to cleanse and purify a space, promoting clarity and positive energy.

5. Wood Sorrel: Wood sorrel is a plant associated with luck, happiness, and positive change. It can be used to attract good fortune and opportunities.

6. Sassafras Root Bark: Sassafras is linked to purification, empowerment, and connecting with ancestral wisdom. It can be used to purify your space and connect with your roots.

Deep Fried and Dirt Grown Candle Dressing Oil

Ingredients:

1. Bacon Grease: Bacon grease is associated with the element of fire and can symbolize transformation, warmth, and vitality. This is the base oil that you'll use to steep the plant product in

2. Sassafras Leaves or Root: Sassafras is a Southern herb with connections to healing, purification, and protection. It's often used for spiritual cleansing and enhancing one's personal power.

3. Spanish Moss: Spanish moss is a distinctive Southern plant associated with mysticism and hidden knowledge. It can be used to enhance psychic abilities, dreamwork, and divination.

4. Honeysuckle Flowers: Honeysuckle represents love, attraction, and the sweetness of life. It can be used to draw positive energies and enhance relationships.

5. Moonshine (or High-Proof Alcohol): Moonshine, being a strong and distilled spirit, can represent the element of water and emotions. It can be used to amplify the magical properties of the other ingredients. Add the moonshine away from any heat source.

Manifestation Oil

Ingredients:

1. Gold Leaf or Gold Flake: Gold symbolizes abundance, success, and the sun's energy. It can be used to enhance the manifestation of prosperity and positive outcomes.

2. Bay Leaf: Bay leaves are associated with victory, achievement, and protection. They can help you manifest your desires while shielding your intentions from negativity.

3. Patchouli Essential Oil: Patchouli is known for its grounding and

attracting properties. It can help you manifest your goals while keeping you rooted in the present moment.

4. Citrine Crystal: Citrine is a stone of abundance and manifestation. It can amplify your intentions and draw positive energy toward your goals.

5. Olive Oil (as a carrier oil): Olive oil is often used as a base for manifestation oils due to its associations with abundance, peace, and prosperity.

Spring Incense

Ingredients:

1. Violet Flowers: Representing spring's arrival and rebirth, violet flowers are associated with love, protection, and healing. They can help you connect with the energies of the season and promote positive changes.

2. Lemongrass: Lemongrass is known for its cleansing and purifying properties. It can help remove stagnant or negative energies, making it perfect for spring cleaning, both physically and spiritually.

3. Dandelion Leaf: Dandelion leaves symbolize wishes and transformation. They can be used to help manifest your desires and goals as you embrace the fresh start of spring.

4. Mugwort: Mugwort is often associated with divination and enhancing psychic abilities. It can help you tap into the intuitive energies of the season and gain clarity about your path forward.

5. Nettle Leaf: Nettle leaf is linked to protection and warding off negative influences. It can help create a shield of positive energy as you step into the new season.

Summer Incense

Ingredients:

1. Dried Honeysuckle Flowers: Associated with love, passion, and attracting positive energies. It's also known for its ability to promote psychic awareness and enhance intuition.

2. Dried Blackberry Leaves: Symbolizes protection, healing, and prosperity. It's believed to ward off negative energies and promote health and wealth.

3. Frankincense Resin: Adds a base to your incense, representing purification, spirituality, and consecration. It's commonly used in rituals to connect with the divine.

4. Rose Petals: Brings in the energy of love, romance, and emotional healing. It's often used for spells related to matters of the heart.

5. Lavender Flowers: Known for its calming and purifying properties. Lavender is used for relaxation, peace, and promoting a harmonious environment.

Autumn Incense

Ingredients:

1. Acorn Powder: Acorns symbolize potential and strength. Acorn powder is associated with protection, prosperity, and personal growth.

2. Apple Peel: Apples represent wisdom, abundance, and the harvest. Apple peel can be used for divination, enhancing intuition, and attracting financial blessings.

3. Oak Bark: Oak is a powerful tree associated with strength, endurance, and protection. Oak bark can help you ground your energy and provide a shield against negative influences.

4. Cinnamon: Cinnamon is linked to abundance, warmth, and com-

fort. It can be used for attracting wealth and prosperity, as well as adding a cozy ambiance to your autumn rituals.

5. Nutmeg: Nutmeg is a spice of transformation and spiritual insight. It can aid in releasing old patterns and connecting with your inner wisdom.

Winter Incense

Ingredients:

1. Pine Needles: Pine is a symbol of endurance, purification, and protection. Pine needles can help cleanse and protect your space during the winter months.

2. Juniper Berries: Juniper is associated with banishing negative energies and promoting spiritual growth. It's often used for purification and removing obstacles.

3. Myrrh Resin: Myrrh represents transformation, healing, and spiritual connection. It's a resin known for its sacred and purifying properties.

4. Clove: Clove is linked to abundance, protection, and love. It can help attract positive energy and warmth during the colder months.

5. Orange Peel: Oranges are associated with joy, abundance, and good fortune. Orange peel can bring a sense of happiness and positivity to your winter rituals.

Fairytale/Story Writing Incense

Ingredients:

1. Dried Rose Petals: Symbolizing love and beauty, rose petals add a romantic and enchanting aroma to your fairytale incense.

2. Lavender Buds: Lavender brings a sense of calm and relaxation, making it perfect for invoking a dreamy fairytale atmosphere.

3. Frankincense Resin: Known for its connection to spirituality, frankincense adds a touch of mysticism to the incense.

4. Myrrh Resin: Myrrh has a deep, earthy scent that enhances the sense of ancient magick and wisdom.

5. Sandalwood Chips or Powder: Sandalwood provides a grounding and woody base note to the incense.

6. Dried Orange Peel: For a hint of citrusy sweetness and a touch of brightness.

7. Cinnamon Sticks: Cinnamon adds warmth and a bit of spice to the blend.

8. Dried apple peels: In Celtic mythology and folklore, They were believed to be portals to the Otherworld and were associated with immortality, youthfulness, and wisdom.

9. Old book fragrance oil: To spark remembrance and fantasy.

Joy Incense

Ingredients:

1. Orange Peel: Dried orange peel adds a bright and uplifting citrus scent, symbolizing joy and positivity.

2. Lemon Verbena Leaves: Lemon verbena is known for its fresh and zesty aroma, which can evoke feelings of happiness and contentment.

3. Lavender Buds: Lavender brings a sense of calm and relaxation, balancing the energetic qualities of joy.

4. Rosemary: Rosemary has a crisp, herbal scent that can invigorate the senses and promote a sense of well-being.

5. Frankincense Resin: Frankincense is often associated with spiritual connection and can add depth to the incense blend.

6. Copal Resin: Copal resin has a sweet and uplifting fragrance, making it a perfect addition for joy incense.

Curse Breaking Incense

Ingredients:

1. Frankincense resin (2 parts): Frankincense has been used for centuries in spiritual and ritual practices. It is associated with purification, protection, and dispelling negative energy. In this incense, it serves as a powerful purifying agent to cleanse your space and break the curse's hold.

2. Myrrh resin (1 part): Myrrh, like frankincense, has a long history of use in spiritual ceremonies. It represents the shedding of old, negative energies and attachments. Myrrh helps to cut ties with negativity and is particularly effective in curse-breaking rituals.

3. Sandalwood powder or resin (1 part): Sandalwood is known for its calming and grounding properties. It brings a sense of peace and tranquility to the ritual, helping you stay centered and focused on your intention.

4. Clove buds (1 part): Cloves are believed to have protective qualities. They can help to repel negative energies and curses. Cloves also add a touch of fiery energy to the incense, aiding in the breaking of the curse.

5. Rosemary leaves (1 part): Rosemary is associated with purification, clarity, and cleansing. It helps to remove any residual negative energy and promotes clarity of thought, which can be important when working to break a curse.

6. Sea Salt (a pinch): Sea salt is a potent purifier. It's often used to create protective circles or barriers. In this incense, a pinch of sea salt adds an extra layer of protection and purification.

Incense blend to Combat Fear

Ingredients:

1. 1 part Dragon's Blood resin: Dragon's Blood resin is known for its strong protective and empowering properties. It can help you face fear

head-on.

2. 1 part Mugwort leaves: Mugwort is often used in divination and dream work. It can help you gain insight into the source of your fears and find the courage to confront them.

3. 1 part Frankincense resin: Frankincense has a calming and grounding effect, which can help alleviate anxiety and promote a sense of inner peace in the face of fear.

4. 1 part Cinnamon bark or chips: Cinnamon adds a touch of fiery energy and empowerment to the blend, encouraging you to overcome fear.

5. 1 part Calendula petals: Calendula represents bravery and protection. It can help create a shield of courage around you.

Incense Blend for Encouragement

Ingredients:

1. 2 parts Rosemary leaves: Rosemary is associated with mental clarity and motivation. It can help you stay focused on your goals.

2. 1 part Patchouli leaves: Patchouli is known for its grounding and uplifting qualities. It can boost self-assurance and determination.

3. 1 part Bergamot peel (dried and grated): Bergamot is uplifting and can promote a sense of joy and encouragement.

4. 1 part Bay leaves: Bay leaves are symbolic of success and achievement. They can help you feel confident in your endeavors.

5. 1 part Cedarwood chips or resin: Cedarwood is grounding and can instill a sense of strength and endurance.

Incense for Rewylding the Spirit

Ingredients:

1. 2 parts Pine resin: Pine is associated with the wild, untamed forest. Its resin can evoke a sense of rugged beauty and connection to nature.

2. 1 part Mugwort leaves: Mugwort is believed to enhance intuition and dreams. It can help you tap into the wild and mystical aspects of your spirit.

3. 1 part Juniper berries: Juniper is known for its protective and purifying qualities. It can create a sense of clarity and strength, like the wilderness.

4. 1 part Oakmoss (dried): Oakmoss has a deep, earthy scent that can transport you to the heart of a forest. It encourages a grounded and primal connection.

5. 1 part Wildflower petals (various types): Wildflowers represent the untamed beauty of nature. Their presence in the blend adds color and a sense of freedom.

Incense for Connecting with the Wyld Animal Allies

Ingredients:

1. 2 parts Pine resin: Pine resin is associated with the forest and wilderness. It represents the spirit of the natural world and can help establish a connection with wildlife.

2. 1 part Cedarwood chips or resin: Cedarwood has a grounding and protective energy, which can create a safe and respectful space for communicating with wildlife.

3. 1 part Yarrow flowers: Yarrow is known for its divinatory properties. It can enhance your ability to receive messages and insights from wildlife.

4. 1 part White sage leaves (dried): White sage is often used for pu-

rification and clarity. It can help you attune to the energies of the animal kingdom.

5. 1 part Oakmoss (dried): Oakmoss has an earthy and primal scent that can deepen your connection with the wilderness.

6. 1 part Mugwort leaves: Mugwort is believed to enhance intuition and dreams. It can help you tap into the wild and mystical aspects of your spirit.

7. 1 part Juniper berries: Juniper is known for its protective and purifying qualities. It can create a sense of clarity and strength, like the wilderness.

8. 1 part Wildflower petals (various types): Wildflowers represent the untamed beauty of nature. Their presence in the blend adds color and a sense of freedom.

Incense Blend for Seeing Beyond the Surface

Ingredients:

1. 2 parts Frankincense resin: Frankincense is often used for its meditative and spiritual properties. It can help open your mind to deeper understanding.

2. 1 part Damiana leaves: Damiana is associated with psychic abilities and enhanced perception. It can aid in seeing beyond the ordinary.

3. 1 part Bay leaves: Bay leaves are connected to wisdom and intuition. They can help you access deeper layers of knowledge.

4. 1 part Lavender buds: Lavender promotes calmness and clarity, which can be beneficial for gaining insight.

5. 1 part Star Anise seeds: Star Anise is linked to mysticism and psychic awareness. It can help you see things from different perspectives.

Incense Blend to Reawaken the Magick Within You:

Ingredients:

1. 2 parts Dragon's Blood resin: Dragon's Blood is associated with power, protection, and transformation. It can ignite the fire of your inner magic.

2. 1 part Mugwort leaves: Mugwort is known for enhancing intuition and psychic abilities. It can help you access the hidden realms of magic within yourself.

3. 1 part Cinnamon bark (ground): Cinnamon adds warmth and energy to the blend, infusing it with vitality and magical potency.

4. 1 part Sandalwood powder or resin: Sandalwood is grounding and can help you harness your magical energies in a balanced way.

5. 1 part Lavender buds: Lavender promotes clarity, calmness, and spiritual insight, making it easier to connect with your inner magic.

6. 2 parts Frankincense resin: Frankincense is often used for its meditative and spiritual properties. It can help open your mind to deeper understanding.

7. 1 part Damiana leaves: Damiana is associated with psychic abilities and enhanced perception. It can aid in seeing beyond the ordinary.

8. 1 part Bay leaves: Bay leaves are connected to wisdom and intuition. They can help you access deeper layers of knowledge.

9. 1 part Star Anise seeds: Star Anise is linked to mysticism and psychic awareness. It can help you see things from different perspectives.

Incense Blend To Help Reignite Magickal Passion:

Ingredients:

1. 2 parts Dragon's Blood resin: Dragon's Blood is associated with power, protection, and transformation. It can ignite your magical fire and determination.

2. 1 part Damiana leaves: Damiana is believed to enhance psychic abilities and passion. It can help you reconnect with the spiritual aspects of your practice.

3. 1 part Ginger root (dried and powdered): Ginger adds a fiery and dynamic energy to the blend, rekindling your passion.

4. 1 part Rose petals: Roses symbolize love, desire, and beauty. They can evoke a deep emotional connection to your magical path.

5. 1 part Cinnamon bark (ground): Cinnamon adds warmth and vitality to the blend, infusing it with energy.

Recipe for "Hearth and Home Incense"

Ingredients:

1. Angelica Root: Angelica root is believed to facilitate communication with the spirit world. Its inclusion encourages a connection with departed loved ones and helps create a sacred space for remembrance.

2. Galangal Root: Galangal root is associated with psychic abilities and divination. It enhances your ability to connect with the spiritual realm during moments of reflection.

3. Fennel Seeds: Fennel seeds represent protection and guidance. They are believed to provide a shield of spiritual protection, ensuring that your remembrance is peaceful and respectful.

4. Frankincense Tears: Frankincense adds a purifying and transcendent quality to the blend. It elevates the atmosphere, making it easier to connect with the memories of your loved ones.

5. Dragon's Blood Resin: Dragon's blood resin is linked to strength and

empowerment. Its presence in the blend helps you feel empowered as you remember and honor departed souls.

6. Yarrow Flowers: Yarrow is considered a protective and healing herb. It creates a safe and nurturing environment for your remembrance rituals.

7. Patchouli Leaves: Patchouli is associated with grounding and stability. It anchors your emotions and memories, allowing you to remember with a sense of balance and stability.

SELECTED BIBLIOGRAPHY

Wikipedia contributors, "Haint blue," Wikipedia, The Free Encyclopedia, https://en.wikipedia.org/w/index.php?title=Haint_blue&oldid=1189203657 (accessed February 26, 2018)

Redmoon, AH. "No peaceful warriors!" Gnosis: No. 21, Fall 1991.

Wolfe, Thomas. *You Can't Go Home Again*. New York: Harper & Row, 1940.

Avedon, Barbara, writer. *Bewitched*. Season 1, episode 2, "Be It Ever So Mortgaged." Directed by William Asher, featuring Agnes Moorehead as Endora. Aired September 24, 1964.

www.ingramcontent.com/pod-product-compliance
Lightning Source LLC
Chambersburg PA
CBHW021504090426
42739CB00007B/463